THE BARTENDER'S COMPANION

A Complete Drink Recipe Guide

SECOND EDITION

by

Robert Plotkin
Chief Contributing Editor

P.S.D. Publishing Co.
Tucson, Arizona
1993

JAN '94

OTHER BOOKS BY ROBERT PLOTKIN

Preventing Internal Theft: A Bar Owner's Guide
The Intervention Handbook: The Legal Aspects Of Serving Alcohol
The Commercial Bartender's Training Manual
The Professional Guide To Bartending - 2nd Edition (with Carol Ann Hermansen)

Library of Congress Card Catalog Number:

ISBN 0-945562-11-X

PUBLISHED AND DISTRIBUTED BY:

P. S. D. PUBLISHING COMPANY
P. O. Box 14486
Tucson, Arizona 85732-4486
(602) 747-8131

This book is dedicated to Mark N. Sklar — over 20 years my friend and mentor. R.P.

THE BARTENDER'S COMPANION

A Complete Drink Recipe Guide
Second Edition

TABLE OF CONTENTS

INTRODUCTION

The Bartender's Companion: A Complete Drink Recipe Guide is intended for use behind a commercial bar. Every aspect of this book has been designed with the professional bartender in mind.

What differentiates a commercial drink recipe guide from one meant for home use?

This guide contains commercial recipes that are formulated to be as cost-effective as possible, all the while giving the customer a "good drink." In the commercial realm, a drink's relative alcoholic potency is a major concern for the safety and welfare of the clientele. Therefore, alcohol portioning is a serious consideration when formulating commercial drink recipes.

Drink recipes meant for home use need not take these factors into consideration.

Many recipe guides promote the use of ingredients that are rarely, if ever, found behind the majority of commercial bars, rendering recipes containing these products virtually unusable. The drink recipes contained in this guide are comprised of ingredients that are readily available.

Unlike other recipe guides, The Bartender's Companion is not affiliated with any liquor manufacturer or distributor. As a result, this guide has been compiled without the bias and influence of an outside proprietary interest. The recipes contained herein do not gratuitously promote a specific brand or line of alcoholic products.

The drinks in this reference were carefully selected from countless scores of existing recipes, culling out the essential material using the following criteria:

• Is the recipe in question still a viable commercial recipe? With the passage of time, tastes and preferences change, all of which will have a profound affect on what drinks customers request. Many of the published drink guides contain recipes that have fallen into virtual obscurity and are now all but obsolete. Therefore, if there is a chance that a particular recipe may still be requested, it has been included in this book.

• If the recipe is not necessarily well-known, but would make an excellent choice for a house specialty drink or a bartender's personal recommendation, it also has been included.

• Finally, truly basic drink combinations, such as gin & tonic or Scotch & water, have been omitted as being overtly obvious, and thus inappropriate content for a professional's drink recipe guide.

ALCOHOL MANAGEMENT

Change in societal mores regarding the consumption of alcohol has had a tremendous impact on the food and beverage industry. As a result, it has changed how, when and to whom we serve alcoholic beverages.

The editors of this book advocate moderation in the consumption of alcohol. In addition, we strongly urge responsibility when serving alcohol. The information contained herein is intended for commercial use, with the understanding that certification from an alcohol-awareness program is now the industry norm for servers of alcohol.

Furthermore, we would like to advance the following:

• A "strong drink" is not necessarily a "good drink." Increasing a drink's liquor portion from 1 ounce to 1½ ounces increases both its alcoholic potency and cost by 50%. Over-portioning alcohol is an expensive and liability-ladened practice.

• Recipes appearing in this drink guide may be altered to better meet your establishment's mixology program. For instance, a recipe calling for ¾ ounces of three alcoholic products may be down-scaled to ½ ounce of each. The non-alcoholic products in the recipe would be reduced similarly. Thought should be given to serving the drink in a slightly smaller glass. Reducing products equally is important to attain the same relative flavor and consistency.

• Not all drinks are created equally. For instance, a Martini served straight-up is more potent than one served on-the-rocks. Alcohol is soluble in water and will increase the rate at which ice melts. As a result, melting ice will dilute the drink's alcohol, rendering it less potent.

• Similarly, a blended drink is less potent than one served on-the-rocks. Blending a drink with ice renders it highly diluted. In most instances, the dominant ingredient in a blended drink is water (ice).

• Neat drinks are prepared directly into the glass in which they are served. They are undiluted and high in alcohol concentration. Care should be taken regarding their service.

• Shooters are frequently undiluted by either water or non-alcoholic mixes. In some cases, shooters are minimally diluted by ice during preparation. As a result, shooters and layered cordial drinks are relatively high in alcohol concentration and service should be tempered accordingly.

• Shooters and layered cordials are conventionally consumed in one swallow, thereby dramatically increasing the rate the alcohol is absorbed into the bloodstream. Increased rate of consumption tends to accelerate the onset of intoxication.

• A "Double" highball, containing 2 ounces of liquor instead of the standard one ounce, is more than twice as potent than a two prepared regularly. A "Double" will profoundly impact intoxication. Conversely, a "Tall" highball, one prepared in a tall glass with significantly more mixer, is less potent than the same drink prepared in the regular manner.

COMMERCIAL DRINK RECIPES

The following are explanations for the
POURING INSTRUCTIONS contained
in the drink recipes:

BLEND WITH ICE — pour ingredients along with ice into blender canister, crush contents until homogenized into a smooth, creamy consistency.

BUILD — pour ingredients into the glass in which the drink is to be served in the same sequence listed in the recipe.

BUILD OR STIR — drink may be prepared either by stirring reciped ingredients over ice in mixing glass and straining into chilled glass, or by pouring ingredients directly into the iced glass in which the drink is to be served.

LAYER — To achieve a layered effect, carefully pour ingredients over the back of a bar spoon directly into the glass in same sequence listed in the recipe.

SHAKE & STRAIN — pour drink ingredients along with ice into mixing glass, place mixing tin over glass and shake vigourously; strain contents away into glass. If hand mixing set is not available, prepare recipe in electric up-mixer.

SHAKE OR BLEND — recipe may be prepared either by shaking the contents in a mixing set and straining away from the ice into a chilled glass, or by blending ingredients with ice in an electric blender until drink achieves a smooth, creamy consistency.

STIR & STRAIN — pour ingredients into iced mixing glass, stir with long-handled bar spoon and strain contents away from ice into chilled glass.

ABBEY ROAD...........................*Build*
Coffee mug, heated
¾ oz. Chambord
½ oz. Amaretto di Saronno
½ oz. Kahlua
Fill with hot coffee
Whipped cream optional

ABERDEEN ANGUS.................*Build*
Coffee mug, heated
1½ oz. Scotch
¾ oz. Drambuie
1 tbsp. honey
½ oz. lemon juice
¾ oz. hot water
Lemon wedge garnish

ABSOLUT GRAND......*Shake & Strain*
Cocktail glass, chilled
1½ oz. Absolut Vodka
¾ oz. Grand Marnier
½ oz. fresh lime juice

ABSOLUT SAMARI.................*Build*
Rocks glass, ice
1½ oz. Absolut Citron
½ oz. Triple Sec
Lemon wedge garnish

ABSOLUT TROUBLE......*Shake & Strain*
House specialty glass, chilled
1½ oz. Absolut Citron
1 oz. Grand Marnier
1 oz. orange juice
½ oz. grenadine

ACAPULCO.................*Shake & Strain*
Collins glass, ice
1 oz. Tequila
1 oz. Myers's Jamaican Rum
1 oz. grapefruit juice
3 oz. pineapple juice
Pineapple wedge garnish

ACAPULCO GOLD.................*Build*
Highball glass, ice
¾ oz. Peach Schnapps
¾ oz. Light Rum
Fill with orange juice

ADIOS MOTHER
See ELECTRIC LEMONADE

ADONIS.....................*Stir & Strain*
Cocktail glass, chilled
½ oz. Sweet Vermouth
1½ oz. Dry Sherry
Dash Angostura or Orange bitters
Orange twist garnish

AFFINITY COCKTAIL
.........*Shake & Strain*
Cocktail glass, chilled
½ oz. Dry Vermouth
½ oz. Sweet Vermouth
1½ oz. Scotch
2 dashes Angostura bitters
Lemon twist garnish

AFTERBURNER (1).........*Shake & Strain*
House specialty glass, ice
½ oz. Gin
½ oz. Vodka
½ oz. Rum
½ oz. Tequila
½ oz. Triple Sec
2 oz. sweet 'n' sour
2 oz. cola
Shake and strain
Float ½ oz. 151 proof Rum

AFTERBURNER (2).................*Build*
Sherry glass, chilled
¾ oz. Kahlua
¾ oz. Jägermeister
¼ oz. 151 Rum

AFTER EIGHT........................*Layer*
Presentation shot glass, chilled
⅓ fill Kahlua
⅓ fill Green Creme de Menthe
⅓ fill half & half cream

AFTER FIVE............................*Layer*
Presentation shot glass, chilled
⅓ fill Kahlua
⅓ fill Peppermint Schnapps
⅓ fill Bailey's Irish Cream

AGGRAVATION.....................*Build*
Rocks glass, ice
1½ oz. Scotch
½ oz. Kahlua
½ oz. half & half cream

AIR PIRACY..........................*Build*
Coffee mug, heated
½ oz. Grand Marnier
½ oz. Creme de Grand Marnier
½ oz. Brandy
Fill with hot coffee
Whipped cream garnish

ALABAMA SLAMMER (1).........*Layer*
Presentation shot glass, chilled
⅓ fill Southern Comfort
⅓ fill Sloe Gin
⅓ fill orange juice

ALABAMA SLAMMER (2).........*Build*
Old Fashion glass, ice
1 oz. Amaretto di Saronno
1 oz. Southern Comfort
½ oz. Rose's lime juice
½ oz. grenadine

ALABAMA SLAMMER (3)
............*Shake & Strain*
Collins glass, ice
1½ oz. Vodka
½ oz. Southern Comfort
½ oz. grenadine
1½ oz. sweet 'n' sour
1½ oz. orange juice

ALABAMA SLAMMER (4).........*Build*
Bucket glass, ice
1 oz. Southern Comfort
¾ oz. Amaretto di Saronno
½ oz. Sloe Gin
Fill with orange juice
Note: *Above recipe often reproportioned as a shooter.*

ALABAMA SLAMMER (5)
............*Shake & Strain*
Rocks glass, chilled
½ oz. Southern Comfort
½ oz. Amaretto di Saronno
½ oz. Sloe Gin
¼ oz. orange juice
¼ oz. sweet 'n' sour
¼ oz. Seven-up

ALASKA.....................*Stir & Strain*
Cocktail glass, chilled
1½ oz. Gin
½ oz. Yellow Chartreuse
½ oz. Dry Sherry
Lemon twist garnish

ALASKAN ICED TEA
See ICED TEA, ALASKAN

ALASKAN QUAALUDE
See QUAALUDE, ALASKAN

ALEXANDER THE GREAT
.........*Shake or Blend*
Cocktail glass, chilled
1 oz. Metaxa Five Star Brandy
½ oz. Brown Creme de Cacao
1½ oz. half & half cream
Nutmeg garnish

ALICE IN WONDERLAND (1)
See A.M.F.

ALICE IN WONDERLAND (2)
...............*Stir & Strain*
Presentation shot glass, chilled
¾ oz. Tia Maria
¾ oz. Grand Marnier
¾ oz. El Tesoro Muy Añejo Tequila

ALMOND JOY.......................*Build*
Rocks glass, ice
1½ oz. Amaretto di Saronno
½ oz. Brown Creme de Cacao
½ oz. half & half cream

ALPINE GLOW............*Shake & Strain*
Collins glass, ice
1½ oz. Brandy
1½ oz. Amber Rum
½ oz. Triple Sec
2 oz. sweet 'n' sour
2 dashes grenadine
Lemon twist garnish

AMARETTO CRUISE
...............*Blend with ice*
House specialty glass
1 oz. Amaretto di Saronno
½ oz. Peach Schnapps
½ oz. Bacardi Light Rum
1 oz. sweet 'n' sour
1 oz. half & half cream
2 oz. orange juice
2 oz. cranberry juice

AMARETTO PIÑA COLADA
See PIÑA COLADA, AMARETTO

AMBER CLOUD.....................*Build*
Brandy snifter, heated
1½ oz. V.S. Cognac
½ oz. Galliano

AMBROSIA.............................*Build*
Champagne glass, chilled
½ fill fresh apricot puree
½ fill Champagne

AMBUSH.............................*Build*
Coffee mug, heated
1 oz. Bushmill's Irish Whiskey
1 oz. Amaretto di Saronno
Fill with hot coffee
Whipped cream garnish

AMERICAN DREAM.................*Build*
Presentation shot glass, chilled
¼ fill Kahlua
¼ fill Amaretto di Saronno
¼ fill Chocolate Schnapps
¼ fill Frangelico

AMERICAN GRAFITTI
............*Shake & Strain*

Bucket glass, ice
¾ oz. Bacardi Light Rum
½ oz. Bacardi Black Label Rum
½ oz. Sloe Gin
½ oz. Southern Comfort
¼ oz. Rose's lime juice
1½ oz. pineapple juice
1½ oz. sweet 'n' sour

AMERICANO...........................*Build*
Rocks glass, ice
l oz. Campari Aperitivo
l oz. Sweet Vermouth
Lemon twist garnish

AMERICANO HIGHBALL......*Build*
Highball glass, ice
¾ oz. Campari Aperitivo
¾ oz. Sweet Vermouth
Fill with club soda
Lemon twist garnish

A.M.F....................................*Build*
a.k.a. DALLAS ALICE,
ALICE IN WONDERLAND (1)
Brandy snifter, ice optional
¾ oz. Tia Maria
¾ oz. Grand Marnier
¾ oz. Cuervo Especial Tequila

ANCIENT MARINER...............*Build*
Brandy snifter, ice optional
1 oz. Grand Marnier
1 oz. Bacardi Gold Reserve Rum

ANDALUSIA........................*Build*
Brandy snifter, ice optional
1½ oz. Amber Rum
½ oz. V.S. Cognac
½ oz. Dry Sherry
Dash Angostura bitters optional
Lemon twist garnish

ANGEL'S KISS ....*Layer*
a.k.a. ANGEL'S TIP
Cordial or pousse café glass
¾ fill Brown Creme de Cacao
¼ fill half & half cream

APPENDECTOMY......*Shake & Strain*
Cocktail glass, chilled
1 oz. Gin
½ oz. Grand Marnier
1½ oz. sweet 'n' sour

APPENDICITIS............*Shake & Strain*
Cocktail glass, chilled
1 oz. Gin
½ oz. Triple Sec
1½ oz. sweet 'n' sour

APPETIZER...............*Shake & Strain*
Cocktail glass, chilled
¾ oz. Gin
¾ oz. Dubonnet
1½ oz. orange juice
Dash Angostura bitters

APPLE BRANDY COOLER
............*Shake & Strain*
Collins glass, ice
1 oz. Brandy
1 oz. Light Rum
4 oz. apple juice
Shake and strain
Float ½ oz. Myers's Jamaican Rum
Lime wedge garnish

APPLE CART...............*Shake & Strain*
Cocktail glass, chilled
1 oz. Calvados
½ oz. Triple Sec
1½ oz. sweet 'n' sour

APPLE COOLER........................*Build*
Collins glass, ice
1¼ oz. Apple Schnapps
½ oz. Vodka
2 oz. cranberry juice
Fill with club soda

APPLE COLLINS
See JACK COLLINS

APPLE GRAND MARNIER......*Build*
Cappuccino cup, heated
¾ oz. Grand Marnier
¾ oz. Calvados
¾ oz. V.S. Cognac
Fill with hot espresso coffee
Top with frothed milk

APPLE MARGARITA
See MARGARITA, APPLE

APPLE STING........................*Build*
Brandy snifter, ice optional
1½ oz. Calvados
½ oz. Peppermint Schnapps

APPLE TODDY.....................*Build*
Coffee mug, heated
1 oz. Apple Jack or Calvados
½ oz. simple syrup
Fill with hot apple cider
Nutmeg garnish

APPLE WORKS........................*Build*
Coffee mug, heated
¾ oz. Bacardi Light Rum
½ oz. Myers's Jamaican Rum
½ oz. Apple Schnapps
½ fill warm cranberry juice
½ fill warm apple cider

APRÉS SKI.............................*Build*
Coffee mug, heated
1 oz. Apple Schnapps
¾ oz. Brandy
Fill with hot apple cider
Cinnamon stick garnish

APRICOT BRANDY FRAPPÉ
See FRAPPÉ, APRICOT BRANDY

APRIL IN PARIS........................*Build*
Champagne glass, chilled
Swirl and coat inside of glass with
1 oz. Grand Marnier
Fill with Champagne
Orange twist garnish

ARTIFICIAL INTELLIGENCE
............*Shake & Strain*
House specialty glass, ice
¾ oz. Myers's Jamaican Rum
¾ oz. Bacardi Light Rum
¾ oz. Bacardi Black Label Rum
¾ oz. Malibu Rum
½ oz. fresh lime juice
3 oz. pineapple juice
Shake and strain
Float ½ oz. Midori
Fresh fruit garnish

ASPEN COFFEE........................*Build*
Coffee mug, heated
½ oz. Kahlua
½ oz. Bailey's Irish Cream
½ oz. Frangelico
Fill with hot coffee
Whipped cream garnish

AUGUST MOON.....................*Build*
Presentation shot glass, chilled
⅓ fill Triple Sec
⅓ fill Amaretto di Saronno
⅓ fill orange juice
Whipped cream garnish

B-52..*Layer*
Cordial or presentation shot glass
⅓ fill Kahlua
⅓ fill Bailey's Irish Cream
⅓ fill Grand Marnier

BABY GRAND COCKTAIL......*Build*
Brandy snifter, heated
¾ oz. Benedictine & Brandy (B & B)
½ oz. Creme de Grand Marnier

BACARDI COCKTAIL...*Shake & Strain*
Cocktail glass, chilled
1 oz. Bacardi Light Rum
1½ oz. sweet 'n' sour
½ oz. grenadine

BAHAMA MAMA.........*Shake & Strain*
Collins glass, ice
1 oz. Light Rum
3 oz. pineapple juice
Shake and strain
Float ½ oz. Myers's Jamaican Rum
Float ½ oz. 151 proof Rum

BAILEY'S COMET...................*Build*
Rocks glass, ice
1½ oz. Stolichnaya Vodka
½ oz. Bailey's Irish Cream

BAILEY'S EXPRESS.....................*Build*
Coffee mug, heated
1¼ oz. Bailey's Irish Cream
Fill with hot espresso coffee
Whipped cream garnish optional

BAILEY'S FIZZ...........................*Build*
Highball glass, ice
1 oz. Bailey's Irish Cream
Fill with club soda

BAILEY'S MINT KISS...............*Build*
Coffee mug, heated
¾ oz. Bailey's Irish Cream
¾ oz. Kahlua
¾ oz. Rumple Minze Schnapps
Fill with hot coffee
Whipped cream garnish optional

BALALAIKA...............*Shake & Strain*
Cocktail glass, chilled
1 oz. Vodka
½ oz. Triple Sec
1½ oz. sweet 'n' sour
Lime wedge garnish

BALASHI BREEZE.........*Blend with ice*
House specialty glass, chilled
1½ oz. Midori
½ oz. Blue Curaçao
½ oz. Red Curaçao
½ oz. Light Rum
2½ oz. coconut syrup
4 oz. pineapple juice

BALL BEARING.......................*Build*
Presentation shot glass, chilled
½ fill Cherry Marnier
½ fill Champagne

BALL JOINT............*Shake & Strain*
Coupette glass, chilled
1 oz. Absolut Vodka
¾ oz. Grand Marnier
3 oz. orange juice

BAM BE................................*Layer*
Cordial or presentation shot glass, chilled
⅓ fill Tia Maria
⅓ fill Bailey's Irish Cream
⅓ fill B. & B. Liqueur

BANANA COW............*Blend with ice*
House specialty glass
1½ oz. Myers's Jamaican Rum
3 oz. milk
½ oz. simple syrup
1 ripe banana
Banana slice garnish

BANANA DAIQUIRI
See DAIQUIRI, FRUIT

BANANA FROST.........*Blend with ice*
House specialty glass
1 oz. Amaretto di Saronno
1 ripe banana
1–2 scoops vanilla or banana ice cream
1 oz. half & half cream
Banana slice garnish

BANANA MARGARITA
See MARGARITA, FRUIT

BANANA POPSICKLE
............*Blend with ice*
House specialty glass, chilled
1 oz. Creme de Banana
1½ oz. orange juice
1 oz. half & half cream
1 ripe banana

BANANA RUM FRAPPÉ
See FRAPPÉ, BANANA RUM

BANANA SANDWICH...............*Layer*
a.k.a. MONKEY'S LUNCH
Presentation shot glass, chilled
⅓ fill Kahlua
⅓ fill Creme de Banana
⅓ fill Myers's Rum Cream

BANANAS BARBADOS
...............*Blend with ice*
House specialty glass, chilled
1 oz. Mount Gay Eclipse Rum
1 oz. Myers's Jamaican Rum
½ oz. Creme de Banana
2 oz. sweet 'n' sour
1 ripe banana
Blend with ice
Float ½ oz. Myers's Jamaican Rum

BANANA SPLIT...............*Blend with ice*
House specialty glass, chilled
¾ oz. White Creme de Menthe
¾ oz. White Creme de Cacao
¾ oz. Creme de Banana
1–2 scoops strawberry ice cream
Whipped cream garnish

BANILLA BOAT............*Blend with ice*
House specialty glass, chilled
1 oz. B. & B. Liqueur
¾ oz. Creme de Banana
1-2 scoops vanilla ice cream
Blend with ice
Float ½ oz. Chambord
Banana slice garnish

BANSHEE......................*Shake or Blend*
Cocktail glass, chilled
½ oz. Creme de Banana
½ oz. White Creme de Cacao
2 oz. half & half cream
Banana slice garnish optional

BARBARY COAST............*Shake & Strain*
Cocktail glass, chilled
¾ oz. Scotch
¾ oz. Gin
¾ oz. White Creme de Menthe
¾ oz. half & half cream

BAT BITE...............................*Build*
Highball glass, ice
1 oz. Bacardi Black Label Rum
Fill with cranberry juice

BATIDA................................*Build*
Bucket glass, ice
1½ oz. Sambista Cachaça
½ fill orange juice
½ fill pineapple juice

BAY AREA GARTER....................*Build*
Coffee mug, heated
½ oz. Kahlua
½ oz. Truffles Chocolate Liqueur
½ oz. Frangelico
½ oz. Hershey's chocolate syrup
Fill with hot coffee
Whipped cream garnish

BAYBREEZE.........................*Build*
a.k.a. DOWNEASTER
Highball glass, ice
1 oz. Vodka
½ fill cranberry juice
½ fill pineapple juice

BEACHCOMBER (1).........*Shake & Strain*
Collins glass, ice
1½ oz. Light Rum
½ oz. Triple Sec
½ oz. Maraschino Liqueur
½ oz. Rose's lime juice
1½ oz. sweet 'n' sour

BEACHCOMBER (2).........*Shake & Strain*
Cocktail glass, chilled
1½ oz. Light Rum
½ oz. Triple Sec
½ oz. grenadine
1 oz. sweet 'n' sour
Lime wheel garnish

BEACH BLONDE............*Shake & Strain*
House specialty glass, ice
1 oz. Bacardi Light Rum
1 oz. Amaretto di Saronno
½ oz. grenadine
½ oz. Rose's lime juice
Shake and strain
Fill with orange juice
Splash Seven-up

BEAM ME UP, SCOTTIE............*Layer*
Presentation shot glass, chilled
⅓ fill Kahlua
⅓ fill Creme de Banana
⅓ fill Bailey's Irish Cream

BEARING STRAIT............*Stir & Strain*
Cocktail glass, chilled
1½ oz. Stolichnaya Cristall Vodka
½ oz. Grand Marnier
½ oz. Rose's lime juice
Lime wedge garnish

BEAUTIFUL THING.................*Build*
Rocks glass, ice
¾ oz. Rumple Minze Schnapps
¾ oz. Bailey's Irish Cream

BEAUTY AND THE BEAST
........................*Build*
Brandy snifter, heated
¾ oz. Benedictine & Brandy (B & B)
¾ oz. Opal Nera Sambuca

BEER BUSTER..........................*Build*
Beer glass or mug, chilled
1 oz. Vodka
2-3 dashes Tabasco sauce
Fill with draft beer

BEE'S KNEES...............*Shake & Strain*
Cocktail glass, chilled
1 oz. Gin
½ oz. honey
1½ oz. sweet 'n' sour

BELINI (BELLINI).....................*Build*
Champagne glass, chilled
½ fill fresh peach puree
½ fill Champagne

BENEDICTINE & BRANDY............*Build*
a.k.a. B. & B.
Cordial glass or brandy snifter, heated
½ fill Benedictine D.O.M.
½ fill Brandy

BERLIN WALL..........................*Build*
Rocks glass, ice
1½ oz. Vodka
½ oz. Bailey's Irish Cream

BERRY NEW SANGRIA (Serves 6-8)
........................*Punch*
Wine goblet or house specialty glass, ice
Prepare in a 2 liter pitcher (or larger)
1 (750ml) bottle dry red wine
2½ oz. Peach Schnapps
16 oz. cran-raspberry juice
3 oz. sweetened raspberry puree
3 oz. sweetened strawberry puree
1½ oz. grapefruit juice
1½ oz. orange juice
2 oz. sweet 'n' sour
Orange, lemon & lime wheels garnish
Mix ingredients in large pitcher or carafe. Refrigerate for 2-3 hours. Serve with ice & fresh fruit garnish.

BETSY ROSS...............*Stir & Strain*
Cocktail glass, chilled
1 oz. Brandy
1 oz. Port
½ oz. Triple Sec
Dash Angostura bitters

BETTY GRABLE......................*Build*
Coffee mug, heated
½ oz. Amaretto di Saronno
½ oz. Bacardi Light Rum
½ oz. Chambord
Fill with hot apple cider
Whipped cream and cinnamon stick garnish

BETWEEN THE SHEETS
............*Shake & Strain*
Collins or bucket glass, ice
l oz. Brandy
½ oz. Triple Sec
½ oz. Light Rum
1½ oz. sweet 'n' sour

BEVERLY HILLBILLY...............*Layer*
Sherry glass, chilled
½ fill Goldwasser
½ fill Jägermeister

BIBLE BELT...............*Shake & Strain*
Cocktail glass, chilled
1 oz. Southern Comfort
½ oz. Triple Sec
1½ oz. sweet 'n' sour
Lime wedge garnish

BIG CHILL..................*Blend with ice*
House specialty glass
1½ oz. Bacardi Black Label Rum
1 oz. coconut cream
1 oz. cranberry juice
1 oz. orange juice
1 oz. pineapple juice
Pineapple wedge and cherry garnish

BIKINI LINE...........................*Build*
Presentation shot glass, chilled
⅓ fill Tia Maria
⅓ fill Chambord
⅓ fill Vodka

BLACK AND TAN..................*Build*
Ale or beer glass, chilled
½ fill draught Stout
½ fill draught Ale

BLACK BEARD'S TREASURE
............*Blend with ice*
House specialty glass, chilled
2 oz. Captain Morgan's Spiced Rum
2 oz. raspberry puree
2 oz. sweet 'n' sour

BLACK CAT...........................*Build*
Bucket glass, ice
1½ oz. Cherry Schnapps
½ oz. Vodka
½ fill witlh cranberry juice
½ fill with cola

BLACK-EYED SUSAN...............*Build*
a.k.a. YELLOW JACKET,
KENTUCKY SCREWDRIVER
Highball glass, ice
l oz. Bourbon
Fill with orange juice

BLACK GOLD MARGARITA
See MARGARITA, BLACK GOLD

BLACK JACK...........................*Build*
Coffee mug, heated
1 oz. Jack Daniel's
1 oz. Rumple Minze Schnapps
Fill with hot coffee

BLACK JAMAICAN.................*Build*
Rocks glass, ice
1½ oz. Myers's Jamaican Rum
½ oz. Tia Maria

BLACK MASS...........................*Layer*
Presentation shot glass, chilled
⅓ fill Kahlua
⅓ fill Sambuca
⅓ fill Bacardi Black Label Rum

BLACK N' BLUE...............*Stir & Strain*
Cocktail glass, chilled
1 oz. Black Death Vodka
½ oz. Blue Curaçao
½ oz. cranberry juice
Lime wedge garnish

BLACK RUBY........................*Build*
Coffee mug, heated
¾ oz. Opal Nera Sambuca
½ oz. Tuaca
   Pinch of sugar, cinnamon, lemon
   and orange zest
Fill with hot coffee

BLACK RUSSIAN.....................*Build*
Rocks glass, ice
1½ oz. Vodka
½ oz. Kahlua

BLACK STOCKINGS.........*Stir & Strain*
Cocktail glass, chilled
2 oz. Black Death Vodka
¼ oz. Chambord
Lemon twist garnish

BLACK VELVET..........................*Build*
Tankard or beer glass, chilled
½ fill draught Stout
½ fill Champagne

BLACK VELVETEEN..................*Build*
Tankard or beer glass, chilled
½ fill draught Stout
½ fill hard apple cider

BLACK WATCH........................*Build*
Rocks glass, ice
1½ oz. Scotch
½ oz. Kahlua
Lemon twist garnish

BLACK WIDOW........................*Build*
Bucket glass, ice
1 oz. Black Death Vodka
1 oz. Amaretti di Saronno
Fill with orange juice
Splash club soda

BLAST FROM THE PAST............*Build*
Cappuccino cup, heated
½ oz. Tia Maria
½ oz. Grand Marnier
½ oz. Cuervo Especial Tequila
¾ fill hot espresso coffee
Top with frothed milk
Shaved chocolate garnish

BLENDED FROG.........*Blend with ice*
House specialty glass
1 oz. Vodka
3 oz. cranberry juice

BLIZZARD (1)............*Blend with ice*
House specialty glass
1½ oz. Bourbon
½ oz. Rose's lime juice
½ oz. grenadine
1½ oz. cranberry juice
Orange slice garnish

BLIZZARD (2)............*Blend with ice*
House specialty glass
¾ oz. Brandy
¾ oz. Kahlua
¾ oz. Bailey's Irish Cream
¾ oz. Myers's Jamaican Rum
½ oz. half & half cream
1-2 scoops vanilla ice cream
Nutmeg garnish

BLOOD & SAND.....................*Build*
Highball glass, ice
¾ oz. Scotch
¾ oz. Cherry Brandy
Fill with orange juice

BLOODHOUND.....................*Build*
Bucket or house specialty glass, ice
Salted rim optional
1 oz. Vodka
1 oz. Dry Sack Sherry
Fill with Bloody Mary mix
Lime wedge and celery garnish

BLOODY BASTARD...............*Build*
Bucket or house specialty glass, ice
Salted rim optional
½ fill Bass Ale
½ fill Bloody Mary mix
Add ½ tbsp. horseradish
Lime wedge and peeled shrimp garnish

BLOODY BRAIN.......................*Build*
Presentation shot glass, chilled
1 oz. Bailey's Irish Cream
1 oz. Peach Schnapps
2-3 drops grenadine

BLOODY BULL........................*Build*
Bucket or house specialty glass, ice
Salted rim optional
1 oz. Vodka
Fill with "Bull Shot"
   (Bloody Mary mix and beef bouillion)
Lime wedge and celery garnish

BLOODY CAESAR....................*Build*
Bucket or house specialty glass, ice
Salted rim optional
1 oz. Vodka
   Fill with Clamato juice or Bleeding Clam
   mix (1½ oz. clam juice in Bloody Mary mix)
Lime wedge and celery garnish

BLOODY CAJUN.......................*Build*
Bucket or house specialty glass, ice
Salted rim optional
1½ oz. Vodka
½ tsp. onion powder
¼ tsp. crushed thyme leaves
Pinch red pepper
2 pinches paprika
Fill with Bloody Mary mix
Lime wedge and celery garnish

BLOODY ITALIAN...................*Build*
Bucket or house specialty glass, ice
Salted rim optional
1½ oz. Vodka
¼ tsp. Italian seasoning
2 pinches garlic powder
2 pinches paprika
Fill with Bloody Mary mix
Lime wedge and celery garnish

BLOODY KAMIKAZE
See KAMIKAZE, BLOODY

BLOODY MARIA.................*Build*
Bucket or house specialty glass, ice
Salted rim optional
1 oz. Tequila
Fill with Bloody Mary mix
Lime wedge and celery garnish

BLOODY MARY......................*Build*
Bucket or house specialty glass, ice
Salted rim optional
l oz. Vodka
Fill with Bloody Mary mix
Lime wedge and celery garnish

BLOODY MARY MIX
46 oz. tomato or V-8 juice
2 oz. Worchestershire sauce
5-6 dashes Tabasco sauce
2 tbsp. celery salt
1 tbsp. black pepper
½ tbsp. salt
2 dashes Angostura bitters
Thoroughly mix ingredients;
taste-test over ice. Keep refrigerated.
   Optional ingredients: prepared
   horseradish; clamato juice; clam juice;
   pureed Mexican salsa; Mexican hot sauce;
   fresh lemon juice; fresh lime juice; beef
   bouillon; seasoned salt; cayenne pepper;
   onion powder; garlic salt or powder;
   diced or pureed jalapeño pepper;
   cilantro; A-1 sauce; chili powder; Italian
   seasonings; paprika; red pepper; crushed
   thyme leaves; ground cumin

BLOODY MARY, GIN...............*Build*
a.k.a. GIN MARY, RED SNAPPER
Bucket or house specialty glass, ice
Salted rim optional
1 oz. Gin
Fill with Bloody Mary mix
Lime wedge and celery garnish

BLOODY MARY, VIRGIN.........*Build*
a.k.a. BLOODY SHAME
Bucket or house specialty glass, ice
Salted rim optional
Fill with Bloody Mary mix
Lime wedge and celery garnish

BLOODY MOOSE.................*Build*
Bucket or house specialty glass, ice
Salted rim optional
1½ oz. Vodka
Fill with Bloody Mary mix
Beef jerky and lime wedge garnish

BLOODY NOSE.....................*Build*
Bucket or house specialty glass, ice
Salted rim optional
1½ oz. Vodka
Fill with Bloody Mary mix
Float raw oyster
Lime wedge and celery garnish

BLOODY RUSSIAN.................*Build*
Presentation shot glass, chilled
½ fill Stolichnaya Pertsovka
½ fill Bloody Mary mix
Lime wedge garnish

BLOODY RUSSIAN BASTARD
........................*Build*
Bucket or house specialty glass, ice
Salted rim optional
½ oz. Stolichnaya Pertsovka
½ oz. Stolichnaya Limonnaya
2 oz. Bass Ale
Fill with Bloody Mary mix
Add ½ tbsp. horseradish
Lime wedge and peeled shrimp garnish

BLOODY TEX-MEX.................*Build*
Bucket or house specialty glass, ice
Salted rim optional
1½ oz. Vodka
½ tsp. chili powder
2 pinches ground cumin
2 pinches paprika
Fill with Bloody Mary mix
Lime wedge and celery garnish

BLOODY WRIGHT.................*Build*
Bucket glass, ice
Salted rim optional
1½ oz. C.J. Wray Rum
Fill with Bloody Mary mix
Lime wedge and celery garnish

BLOW JOB (1).........................*Build*
Presentation shot glass, chilled
½ fill Grand Marnier
½ fill Creme de Grand Marnier
Whipped cream garnish

BLOW JOB (2).........................*Build*
Presentation shot glass, chilled
⅓ fill Grand Marnier
⅓ fill Creme de Banana
⅓ fill Tia Maria
Whipped cream garnish

BLUE ANGEL.........................*Build*
Presentation shot glass, chilled
½ fill Blue Curaçao
½ fill orange juice

BLUE BAYOU (1).......................*Build*
Bucket glass, ice
1½ oz. Vodka
¾ oz. Blue Curaçao
½ fill pineapple juice
½ fill grapefruit juice

BLUE BAYOU (2)............*Blend with ice*
House specialty glass, chilled
1½ oz. Light Rum
1 oz. Blue Curaçao
½ oz. half & half cream
1-2 scoops French vanilla ice cream
Orange slice and cherry garnish

BLUEBERRY TEA........................*Build*
Tea cup or coffee mug, heated
¾ oz. Grand Marnier
¾ oz. Amaretto di Saronno
Fill with hot tea
Lemon wedge garnish

BLUE BLAZER...........................*Build*
Mug or tankard
2 oz. Scotch
¾ oz. honey
¼ oz. lemon juice
2–3 oz. water
  **Combine and bring slowly to boil,
  allowing honey to dissolve before
  serving.**
Note: *Traditionally prepared aflame; this is an
extremely dangerous and highly discouraged
practice.*

BLUE DEVIL.............................*Build*
a.k.a. BLUE MOON
Cocktail glass, chilled
1 oz. Gin
½ oz. Blue Curaçao
1½ oz. sweet 'n' sour

BLUE HAWAII............*Shake or Blend*
Cocktail or house specialty glass, chilled
½ oz. Light Rum
½ oz. Blue Curaçao
½ oz. White Creme de Cacao
1½ oz. half & half cream

BLUE HAWAIIAN.........*Shake & Strain*
Collins glass, ice
1½ oz. Light Rum
½ oz. Blue Curaçao
1½ oz. sweet 'n' sour
1½ oz. pineapple juice
1½ oz. coconut syrup optional
Orange or pineapple garnish

BLUE KAMIKAZE
See KAMIKAZE, BLUE

BLUE KANGAROO.........*Shake & Strain*
House specialty glass, ice
½ oz. Gin
½ oz. Vodka
½ oz. Light Rum
½ oz. Tequila
½ oz. Blue Curaçao
2 oz. sweet 'n' sour
Shake and strain
½ fill Seven-up
½ fill club soda
Lemon wedge garnish

BLUE LADY..................*Shake & Strain*
Cocktail glass, chilled
1½ oz. Bombay Sapphire Gin
½ oz. Blue Curaçao
1½ oz. sweet 'n' sour

BLUE LAGOON........................*Build*
Collins or house specialty glass, ice
1 oz. Blueberry Schnapps
Fill with lemonade
Float ½ oz. Blue Curaçao
Lemon twist garnish

BLUE LEMONADE.....................*Build*
Bucket glass, ice
1½ oz. Absolut Citron
¾ oz. Blue Curaçao
Fill with lemonade

BLUE MARGARITA
See MARGARITA, BLUE

BLUE MARLIN.........*Shake & Strain*
Cocktail glass, chilled
1½ oz. Appleton Estate Jamaican Rum
½ oz. Blue Curaçao
1 oz. fresh lime juice
Lime wheel garnish

BLUE MOON CAFE...............*Build*
Sherry glass, chilled
⅓ fill Blue Curaçao
⅓ fill orange juice
⅓ fill Champagne

BLUE MOON MARGARITA
See MARGARITA, BLUE MOON

BLUE TAIL FLY.........*Shake or Blend*
Cocktail or house specialty glass, chilled
½ oz. White Creme de Cacao
½ oz. Blue Curaçao
2 oz. half & half cream

BLUE WHALE............................*Build*
Bucket glass, ice
1½ oz. Peach Schnapps
¾ oz. Blue Curaçao
Fill with Seven-up

BLUSHING BERRY COOLER
............*Blend with ice*
House specialty glass
1½ oz. Kahlua
4 oz. strawberry puree
or ½ cup frozen strawberries
2½ oz. lowfat milk
2 oz. plain lowfat yogurt
2 oz. frozen orange juice concentrate

BOBBY BURNS................*Stir & Strain*
Cocktail glass, chilled
1½ oz. Scotch
½ oz. Sweet Vermouth
½ oz. Drambuie
Note: *May also be prepared by substituting Benedictine D.O.M. for Drambuie.*

BOBSLEDDER'S BANSHEE
...............*Blend with ice*
House specialty glass, chilled
1 oz. Dr. McGillicuddy's Mentholmint
1 oz. Bailey's Irish Cream
½ oz. half & half cream
1-2 scoops vanilla ice cream
2 chocolate chip cookies
Chocolate chip cookie garnish

BOCCI BALL............................*Build*
Highball glass, ice
1 oz. Amaretto di Saronno
Fill with orange juice
Splash club soda

BOCCI SHOOTER......................*Build*
Presentation shot glass, chilled
½ fill Amaretto di Saronno
½ fill orange juice
Splash club soda

BODY WARMER.....................*Build*
Tea or coffee cup, heated
1¼ oz. Grand Marnier
½ oz. simple syrup optional
Fill with hot tea

BOG FOG.................................*Build*
Highball glass, ice
1 oz. Light Rum
½ fill cranberry juice
½ fill orange juice

BOGS & BUBBLES......................*Build*
Champagne glass, chilled
½ fill cranberry juice
½ fill Champagne

BOILERMAKER........................*Build*
Beer mug and shot glass
Requested whiskey in a shot glass
presented with mug of beer
Note: *A* **DEPTHCHARGE** *is prepared as above, but a shot glass of whiskey is dropped into beer.*

BOMB.........................*Shake & Strain*
House specialty glass, ice
1 oz. Scotch
1 oz. Bourbon
½ oz. 151 Rum
½ oz. Myers's Jamaican Rum
1½ oz. orange juice
1½ oz. pineapple juice
Float ½ oz. grenadine

BOMBAY GRAND......*Shake & Strain*
Cocktail glass, chilled
1 oz. Bombay Sapphire Gin
½ oz. Grand Marnier
1 oz. fresh lemon juice
Orange twist garnish

BOMBAY SPIDER..................*Build*
Bucket glass, ice
1¼ oz. Bombay Sapphire Gin
2-3 dashes Angostura bitters
Fill with ginger ale

BOSOM CARESSER.........*Shake & Strain*
Cocktail glass, chilled
1½ Brandy
½ oz. Triple Sec
3 dashes grenadine
1 egg yolk

BOSS....................................*Build*
Rocks glass, ice
1½ oz. Bourbon
½ oz. Amaretto di Saronno

BOSTON MARTINI
See MARTINI, BOSTON

BOTTOM BOUNCER..................*Build*
Presentation shot glass, chilled
1 oz. Bailey's Irish Cream
1 oz. Butterscotch Schnapps

BRAHMA BULL........................*Build*
Rocks glass, ice
1½ oz. Cuervo Especial Tequila
½ oz. Tia Maria

BRAIN SHOOTER.................*Build*
Presentation shot glass, chilled
¾ oz. Bailey's Irish Cream
½ oz. Peppermint Schnapps
2-3 drops grenadine in center of drink

BRAINSTORM COCKTAIL
................*Stir & Strain*
Cocktail glass, chilled
1½ oz. Irish (or Rye) whiskey
½ oz. Benedictine D.O.M.
½ oz. Dry Vermouth
Orange twist garnish

BRANDY ALEXANDER
............*Shake or Blend*
Cocktail or house specialty glass, chilled
¾ oz. Brandy
¾ oz. Brown Creme de Cacao
1½ oz. half & half cream
Nutmeg garnish

BRANDY EGG NOG (1)
............*Shake & Strain*
Collins glass or goblet, ice
1½ oz. Brandy
4 oz. half & half cream
1 tsp. sugar
2-3 dashes vanilla
1 egg
Nutmeg garnish

BRANDY EGG NOG (2)...............*Build*
Coffee mug, heated
¾ oz. Brandy
¾ oz. Brown Creme de Cacao
Fill with hot milk
Nutmeg garnish

BRANDY GUMP.........*Shake & Strain*
Cocktail glass, chilled
1 oz. Brandy
½ oz. grenadine
1½ oz. sweet 'n' sour

BRANDY MANHATTAN
See **MANHATTAN, BRANDY**

BRASS MONKEY.....................*Build*
Highball glass, ice
½ oz. Light Rum
½ oz. Vodka
Fill with orange juice

BRAVE BULL............................*Build*
Rocks glass, ice
1½ oz. Tequila
½ oz. Kahlua

BRAWNY BROTH.....................*Build*
Coffee mug, heated
1¼ oz. Vodka
Fill with hot beef bouillion
Dash of lemon pepper

BRAZIL.........................*Stir & Strain*
a.k.a. BAHIA
Cocktail glass, chilled
1 oz. Dry Vermouth
1 oz. Dry Sherry
Dash Pernod
Dash Angostura bitters
Lemon twist garnish

BRAZILIAN PIÑA COLADA
See **PIÑA COLADA, BRAZILIAN**

BRONX..........................*Stir & Strain*
Cocktail glass, chilled
1½ oz. Gin
½ oz. Dry Vermouth
½ oz. Sweet Vermouth
½ oz. orange juice

BROOKLYN.....................*Stir & Strain*
Cocktail glass, chilled
½ oz. Dry Vermouth
1½ oz. Bourbon (or Rye whiskey)
Dash Amer Picon or Angostura bitters
Dash Maraschino Liqueur

BROWN SQUIRREL.........*Shake or Blend*
Cocktail or house specialty glass, chilled
½ oz. Amaretto di Saronno
½ oz. Brown Creme de Cacao
2 oz. half & half cream

BRUT 'N BOGS.......................*Build*
Champagne glass, chilled
1 oz. Chambord
½ fill cranberry juice
½ fill Champagne

B-STING.....................*Stir & Strain*
Cocktail glass, chilled
1½ oz. Benedictine & Brandy (B & B)
½ oz. Peppermint Schnapps

BUBBLE GUM............*Shake & Strain*
Presentation shot glass, chilled
½ oz. Southern Comfort
½ oz. Amaretto di Saronno
½ oz. Creme de Banana
½ oz. whole milk
1-2 dashes grenadine

BUCK..........................*Build*
Highball glass, ice
1 oz. requested liquor
Fill with ginger ale
Lemon wedge garnish

BUCKEYE MARTINI
See MARTINI, BUCKEYE

BUCKHEAD ROOTBEER.........*Build*
Highball glass, ice
1¼ oz. Jägermeister
Fill with club soda
Lime wedge garnish

BUCK'S FIZZ
See MIMOSA

BULL AND BEAR............*Stir & Strain*
Cocktail glass, chilled
1½ oz. Bourbon
¾ oz. Triple Sec
¼ oz. grenadine
3–4 dashes Rose's lime juice
Orange slice and cherry garnish

BULLFIGHTER.....................*Layer*
Presentation shot glass, chilled
½ fill Kahlua
½ fill Tequila

BULLFROG (1)..........................*Build*
Highball glass, ice
1 oz. Vodka
Fill with lemonade
Lemon twist garnish

BULLFROG (2)..........................*Build*
Bucket glass, ice
1½ oz. Crystal Comfort
¾ oz. Midori
2½ oz. sweet 'n' sour
Fill with Seven-up

BURGUNDY COCKTAIL
...............*Stir & Strain*
Wine glass, chilled
3 oz. dry red wine
¾ oz. V.S. Cognac
½ oz. Cherry Marnier
Lemon twist garnish

BUSH TICKLER.........*Blend with ice*
House specialty glass
1 oz. Bacardi Black Label Rum
1 oz. Kahlua
¾ oz. Brown Creme de Cacao
½ oz. half & half cream
2 oz. coconut syrup
3 oz. pineapple juice
Pineapple wedge garnish

BUSHWACKER...........*Blend with ice*
House specialty glass
½ oz. Vodka
½ oz. Light Rum
½ oz. Kahlua
½ oz. Amaretto di Saronno
½ oz. Bailey's Irish Cream
½ oz. Frangelico
1 oz. coconut syrup
Pineapple wedge garnish

BUSTED RUBBER.................*Layer*
Presentation shot glass, chilled
⅓ fill Raspberry Schnapps
⅓ fill Bailey's Irish Cream
⅓ fill Grand Marnier

BUTTERFINGER.......................*Layer*
Presentation shot glass, chilled
⅓ fill Truffles Chocolate Liqueur
⅓ fill Butterscotch Schnapps
⅓ fill Bailey's Irish Cream

BUTTERSCOTCH HOP
...............*Blend with ice*
House specialty glass
¾ oz. Butterscotch Schnapps
¾ oz. Kahlua
¾ oz. half & half cream
1–2 scoops vanilla ice cream

BYRRH COCKTAIL............*Stir & Strain*
Cocktail glass, chilled
1 oz. Byrrh
1 oz. Gin
½ oz. Dry Vermouth optional
Lemon twist garnish
  Note: *May also be made using rye whiskey*
  instead of gin.

C. & C....................................*Build*
Brandy snifter, heated
1½ oz. V.S. Cognac
½ oz. Green Chartreuse

CACTUS JUICE.......................*Build*
Bucket glass, ice
1¼ oz. Tequila
¾ oz. Amaretto di Saronno
Fill with sweet 'n' sour
Lime wedge garnish

CACTUS MOON.......................*Build*
Bucket glass, ice
1½ oz. Vodka
½ oz. Triple Sec
½ oz. fresh lemon juice
Fill with lemonade
Lemon wedge garnish

CACTUS ROSE MARGARITA
See MARGARITA, CACTUS ROSE

CADILLAC MARGARITA
See MARGARITA, CADILLAC

CAFÉ AMORE............................*Build*
Coffee mug, heated
½ oz. Truffles Chocolate Liqueur
½ oz. Amaretto di Saronno
½ oz. Tia Maria
½ oz. V.S. Cognac
Fill with hot coffee
Whipped cream garnish

CAFÉ BRÛLOT (Serves two)
........................*Build*
Demitasse cups (2), heated
1 oz. Brandy
1 oz. Triple Sec
Lemon and orange peel spirals
Cinnamon stick
4 whole cloves
1½ cups hot chicory coffee
Heat brandy, Triple Sec, lemon and orange peels in a shallow bowl; ignite mixture; ladle flaming liquid over orange peel; slowly pour hot coffee into bowl to extinguish flame; juice orange juice into mixture, pour into demitasse cups.

CAFÉ CHARLES (Serves two)
........................*Build*
Irish coffee mugs (2), heated
¾ oz. Metaxa 5 Star Brandy
¾ oz. Galliano
¾ oz. Kahlua
Fill with hot coffee
Whipped cream and shaved chocolate garnish
Ignite Metaxa, Brandy and Galliano in glass; pour flaming mixture between glasses; pour in hot coffee to extinguish flame; garnish and serve

CAFÉ CHOCOLATE..................*Build*
Coffee mug, heated
¾ oz. Kahlua
¾ oz. Bailey's Irish Cream
½ oz. Brown Creme de Cacoa
½ oz. Grand Marnier
1½ oz. Hershey's chocolate syrup
Fill with hot coffee
Whipped cream and shaved chocolate garnish

CAFÉ CORRECTO.................*Build*
Coffee mug, heated
1 oz. Brandy
Fill with hot espresso coffee
Whipped cream garnish optional

CAFÉ DIABLO............................*Build*
Coffee mug, heated
¾ oz. V.S. Cognac
¾ oz. Grand Marnier
¾ oz. Sambuca
½ oz. simple syrup
Sprinkle grated orange rind, cloves, cinnamon and allspice
Fill with hot coffee
Orange twist garnish

CAFÉ DUBLIN............................*Build*
Coffee mug, heated
1 oz. Irish Whiskey
1 oz. Irish Mist
½ oz. Kahlua
Fill with hot coffee
Spoon on frothed milk
Dust with powdered cocoa

CAFÉ FOSTER............................*Build*
Coffee mug, heated
1 oz. Bacardi Black Label Rum
½ oz. Creme de Banana
Fill with hot coffee
Vanilla-flavored whipped cream garnish

CAFÉ GATES............................*Build*
Presentation shot glass, chilled
⅓ fill Grand Marnier
⅓ fill Tia Maria
⅓ fill Brown Creme de Cacao

CAFÉ KINGSTON...................*Build*
Coffee mug, heated
½ oz. Myers's Jamaican Rum
½ oz. Bailey's Irish Cream
½ oz. Tia Maria
½ oz. Hershey's chocolate syrup
Fill with hot coffee
Whipped cream garnish

CAFÉ MARGARITA...............*Build*
Coffee mug, heated
¾ oz. Sauza Conmemorativo Tequila
¾ oz. Triple Sec
½ oz. half & half cream
Fill with hot coffee
Whipped cream garnish optional

CAFÉ REGGAE........................*Build*
Coffee mug, heated
½ oz. Tia Maria
½ oz. Bacardi Black Label Rum
½ oz. Brown Creme de Cacao
Fill with hot coffee
Whipped cream garnish optional

CAFÉ ROYALE..........................*Build*
Coffee mug, heated
½ oz. simple syrup optional
1 oz. V.S. Cognac or Brandy
Fill with hot coffee

CAFÉ ST. ARMANDS...............*Build*
Coffee mug, heated
1 oz. Brown Creme de Cacao
½ oz. Licor 43
Fill with hot coffee
Whipped cream garnish

CAIPIRINHA...........................*Build*
Rocks or old fashion glass
4 large lime wedges
¾ oz. simple syrup
2½ oz. Sambista Cachaça
Muddle contents
Add cracked ice

CAIPIRISSMA..........................*Build*
Rocks or old fashion glass
4 large lime wedges
¾ oz. simple syrup
2 ½ oz. Bacardi Light Rum
Muddle contents
Add cracked ice

CAIPIROSHKA.......................*Build*
Rocks or old fashion glass
4 large lime wedges
¾ oz. simple syrup
2½ oz. Vodka
Muddle contents
Add cracked ice

CAJUN MARGARITA
See MARGARITA, CAJUN 1 and 2

CAJUN MARTINI
See MARTINI, CAJUN

CAJUN MIMOSA....................*Build*
Champagne glass, chilled
½ oz. jalapeño juice
½ fill orange juice
½ fill Champagne
Orange wheel and pepper garnish

CALIFORNIA ICED TEA
See ICED TEA, CALIFORNIA

CALIFORNIA LEMONADE
............*Shake & Strain*
Bucket glass, ice
1½ oz. Seagram's 7
1½ oz. sweet 'n' sour
½ oz. Rose's lime juice
½ oz. grenadine
Fill with club soda
Orange slice and cherry garnish

CALIFORNIAN........................*Build*
Highball glass, ice
1 oz. Vodka
½ fill orange juice
½ fill sweet 'n' sour
Splash Seven-up

CALIFORNIA ROOT BEER............*Build*
Highball glass, ice
¾ oz. Kahlua
¾ oz. Galliano
Fill with club soda

CALIFORNIA SCREW...............*Build*
a.k.a. CALIFORNIA SPLIT, DESERT SCREW
Highball glass, ice
1 oz. Vodka
½ fill orange juice
½ fill grapefruit juice

CALYPSO COFFEE.....................*Build*
a.k.a. SPANISH COFFEE
Coffee mug, heated
¾ oz. Light Rum
¾ oz. Tia Maria
Fill with hot coffee
Whipped cream garnish

CALYPSO DAIQUIRI.........*Blend with ice*
House specialty glass
1½ oz. Myers's Jamaican Rum
2½ oz. sweet 'n' sour
½ oz. half & half cream
1 ripe banana
1 tsp. vanilla extract

CALYPSO HIGHWAY.........*Shake & Strain*
House specialty glass, ice
1 oz. Bacardi Black Label Rum
1 oz. Creme de Banana
½ oz. Blue Curaçao
½ oz. coconut syrup
2 oz. pineapple juice
2 oz. orange juice
Shake and strain
Float ½ oz. Nassau Royale
Pineapple wedge and cherry garnish

CAMPARI & SODA...................*Build*
Highball glass, ice
1 oz. Campari Aperitivo
Fill with club soda
Lemon twist garnish

CANADIAN...................*Stir & Strain*
a.k.a. CANADA
Cocktail glass, chilled
1½ oz. Canadian Whisky
½ oz. Triple Sec
2 dashes Angostura bitters
½ oz. simple syrup
1 oz. sweet 'n' sour optional

CANNONBALL.........................*Build*
Bucket glass, ice
2 oz. Pusser's British Navy Rum
1 oz. cranberry juice
1 oz. pineapple juice
1 oz. orange juice
Lime wedge garnish

CANYON SLIDER.....................*Layer*
Presentation shot glass, chilled
½ fill Dr. McGillicuddy's Mentholmint
½ fill Bourbon

CANYON QUAKE.........*Blend with ice*
House specialty glass
¾ oz. Bailey's Irish Cream
¾ oz. Brandy
1 oz. half & half cream

CAPE CODDER.......................*Build*
a.k.a. CAPE COD
Highball glass, ice
. 1 oz. Vodka
Fill with cranberry juice

CAPPA 21..............................*Build*
Cappuccino cup, heated
½ oz. Tia Maria
½ oz. Light Rum
½ oz. Brandy
½ fill with hot espresso coffee
½ fill frothed milk
Shaved chocolate garnish

CAPPO de TUTTI CAPPI............*Build*
Cappuccino cup, heated
½ oz. Tia Maria
½ oz. Brandy
½ oz. Bacardi Black Label Rum
Square of Ghirardelli chocolate
Fill ¾ full with hot espresso coffee
Spoon on frothed milk
Shaved chocolate garnish

CAPPUCCINO...........................*Build*
Coffee mug, heated
½ oz. Brandy
½ oz. White Creme de Cacao
½ oz. Galliano
Fill with hot coffee
Spoon on frothed milk

CAPTAIN'S COOLER.................*Build*
Collins glass, ice
1 oz. Captain Morgan's Spiced Rum
½ oz. Triple Sec
½ oz. Grand Marnier
½ oz. Rose's lime juice
½ oz. cranberry juice
1 oz. orange juice
Shake and strain
Fill with Seven-up

CARIBBEAN BERRY
...........*Blend with ice*
House specialty glass
¾ oz. Light Rum
¾ oz. Amaretto di Saronno
½ oz. Creme de Banana
½ cup strawberries
1½ oz. sweet 'n' sour
Strawberry and banana garnish

CARIBBEAN CRUISE
...........*Blend with ice*
House specialty glass
1 oz. Myers's Jamaican Rum
1 oz. Kahlua
2 oz. coconut syrup
3 oz. pineapple juice
½ oz. half & half cream optional
Pineapple wedge and cherry garnish

CARIBBEAN CHAMPAGNE
.......................*Build*
Champagne glass, chilled
¾ oz. Light Rum
¾ oz. Creme de Banana
Fill with Champagne
Banana and cherry garnish

CARIBBEAN DREAM.................*Build*
Coffee mug, heated
½ oz. Myers's Jamaican Rum
½ oz. Creme de Banana
½ oz. White Creme de Cacao
Fill with hot coffee
Whipped cream garnish

CARIBBEAN GRID LOCK
............*Shake & Strain*
House specialty glass, ice
½ oz. Myers's Jamaican Rum
½ oz. Bacardi Light Rum
½ oz. Mount Gay Eclipse Rum
1½ oz. fresh lime juice
1 oz. orange juice

CARIBE SUNSET.....................*Build*
Presentation shot glass
⅓ fill Chambord
⅓ fill Brown Creme de Cacao
⅓ fill Tia Maria
Splash hot coffee

CARMALITA
See F-16

CATALINA MARGARITA
See MARGARITA, CATALINA

CARTE BLANCHE.....................*Build*
Coffee mug, heated
½ oz. Brandy
½ oz. White Creme de Menthe
½ oz. Chocolate Schnapps
Fill with hot chocolate
Whipped cream garnish topped with
  ½ oz. Green Creme de Menthe

CARTEL BUSTER.....................*Layer*
Presentation shot glass, chilled
⅓ fill Tia Maria
⅓ fill Grand Marnier
⅓ fill Cuervo Especial Tequila

CARTEL SHOOTER.................*Build*
Presentation shot glass, chilled
⅓ fill Chambord
⅓ fill Vodka
Splash grapefruit juice
Splash sweet 'n' sour

C. C. RIDER............................*Build*
Presentation shot glass, chilled
½ fill Chambord
½ fill Champagne

CENSORED ON THE BEACH.........*Build*
Highball glass, ice
1 oz. Peach Schnapps
½ oz. Vodka
½ fill cranberry juice
½ fill orange juice

CHABLIS CHILLER.................*Build*
White wine glass, ice
1 oz. Vodka
½ oz. grenadine
½ oz. fresh lemon juice
Fill with white wine

CHAMBORD DREAM
............*Shake & Strain*
Cocktail or house specialty glass, chilled
½ oz. Chambord
½ oz. Brown Creme de Cacao
2 oz. half & half cream

CHAMBORD REPOSE.................*Build*
Coffee mug, heated
¾ oz. Chambord
½ oz. Brown Creme de Cacao
½ oz. Tia Maria
Fill with hot coffee
Spoon on frothed milk
Shaved chocolate garnish

CHAMPAGNE COCKTAIL............*Build*
Champagne glass, chilled
Sugar cube soaked with Angostura bitters
Fill with Champagne
Lemon twist garnish

CHAMPAGNE FRAMBOISE.........*Build*
Champagne glass, chilled
Fill with Champagne
Float ½ oz. Chambord
Lemon twist garnish

CHAMPAGNE IMPERIAL.........*Build*
Champagne glass, chilled
Angostura bitters soaked sugar cube
½ oz. V.S. Cognac
½ oz. Grand Marnier
Fill with Champagne
Lemon twist garnish

CHAMPAGNE MARSEILLE
............*Shake & Strain*
Champagne glass, chilled
¾ oz. Grand Marnier
¾ oz. Amaretto di Saronno
½ oz. Stolichnaya Vodka
1½ oz. orange juice
Shake and strain
Fill with Champagne

CHAMPAGNE NORMANDY......*Build*
Champagne glass, chilled
1 oz. Calvados
½ oz. simple syrup
2 dashes Angostura bitters
Fill with Champagne
Orange twist garnish

CHAMPS ELYSEES COCKTAIL
............*Shake & Strain*
Cocktail glass, chilled
1 oz. Brandy
½ oz. Benedictine D.O.M.
2 dashes Angostura bitters
1½ oz. sweet 'n' sour

CHARLIE GOODLEG
See FREDDY FUDPUCKER

CHEAP SHADES............*Blend with ice*
House specialty glass, chilled
1 oz. Midori
1 oz. Peach Schnapps
1 oz. sweet 'n' sour
2 oz. orange juice
2 oz. pineapple juice
Blend with ice
Fill with Seven-up

CHEAP SUNGLASSES............*Build*
Bucket glass, ice
1¼ oz. Vodka
½ fill cranberry juice
½ fill Seven-up

CHERRY AMOR............*Shake & Strain*
Champagne glass, chilled
¾ oz. Cherry Marnier
½ oz. Brandy
2 oz. sweet 'n' sour
Shake and strain
Fill with Champagne

CHERRY BEAN......................*Layer*
Cordial or presentation shot glass
½ fill Anisette
½ fill Cherry Brandy

CHERRY BLOSSOM......*Shake & Strain*
Cocktail glass, chilled
1½ oz. Cherry Brandy
1 oz. Brandy
¾ oz. sweet 'n' sour
Dash Triple Sec
Dash grenadine
Cherry garnish

CHERRY BOMB......................*Layer*
Presentation shot glass, chilled
¼ fill Kahlua
¼ fill Creme de Banana
¼ fill Myers's Rum Cream
¼ fill Cherry Schnapps

CHICAGO........................*Stir & Strain*
Champagne glass, chilled
Sugar rim optional
1 oz. Brandy
½ oz. Triple Sec
Dash Angostura bitters
Fill with Champagne
Lemon twist garnish

CHICAGO TIMES....................*Build*
Coffee mug, heated
½ oz. Amaretto di Saronno
½ oz. Tuaca
½ oz. Bailey's Irish Cream
½ fill with hot coffee
½ fill with hot cocoa
Whipped cream garnish topped with ½ oz.
Frangelico and sprinkle of powdered cocoa

CHI-CHI........................*Blend with ice*
House specialty glass
1 oz. Vodka
2 oz. coconut cream syrup
3 oz. pineapple juice
½ oz. half & half cream optional
Pineapple wedge garnish

CHILLER................................*Build*
Highball glass, ice
1 oz. liquor/liqueur
Fill with ginger ale

CHILL-OUT CAFÉ....................*Build*
Coffee mug or glass, ice
½ oz. Kahlua
½ oz. Amaretto di Saronno
½ oz. Brown Creme de Cacao
Fill with iced coffee
Fresh mint sprig garnish

CHIMAYO COCKTAIL
.........*Shake & Strain*
Cocktail or house specialty glass, chilled
1 oz. Sauza Conmemorativo Tequila
½ oz. Creme de Cassis
½ oz. fresh lime juice
3 oz. unfiltered apple cider

CHINACOUT MARGARITA
See MARGARITA, CHINACOUT

CHIP SHOT............................*Build*
Presentation shot glass
⅓ fill Kahlua
⅓ fill Amaretto di Saronno
⅓ fill hot coffee

CHIQUITA PUNCH......*Blend with ice*
House specialty glass
1 oz. Creme de Banana
½ oz. Kahlua
½ oz. Brown Creme de Cacao
¾ oz. grenadine
1½ oz. half & half cream
1½ oz. orange juice
Banana garnish

CHOCOLATE BANANA
...........*Blend with ice*
House specialty glass
1¼ oz. Creme de Banana
1 oz. Hershey's chocolate syrup
1 whole banana
1-2 scoops vanilla ice cream
Whipped cream and shaved chocolate garnish

CHOCOLATE MILK COOLER
...........*Blend with ice*
House specialty glass
1½ oz. Kahlua
8 oz. skim milk
2½ oz. instant nonfat milk
1 tbsp. unsweetened cocoa
1 tsp. vanilla extract
2-3 tsp. sugar
Whipped cream garnish

CHOCOLATE SQUIRREL
...........*Shake or Blend*
Cocktail glass, chilled
½ oz. Amaretto di Saronno
½ oz. Frangelico
½ oz. Brown Creme de Cacao
1½ oz. half & half cream

CINNFUL APPLE.....................*Build*
Highball glass, ice
1 oz. Cinnamon Schnapps
Fill with apple cider

CITRON KAMI
See KAMIKAZE, CITRON

CITRON NEON...........*Blend with ice*
House specialty glass, chilled
1½ oz. Absolut Citron
1 oz. Midori
½ oz. Blue Curaçao
½ oz. Rose's lime juice
2 oz. sweet 'n' sour

CLAM DIGGER.....................*Build*
Bucket glass, ice
Salted rim optional
1½ oz. Gin
2-3 dashes red pepper sauce
Fill with clam juice

CLAM FOGGER......................*Build*
Highball glass, ice
1 oz. Vodka
⅓ fill cranberry juice
⅓ fill grapefruit juice
⅓ fill orange juice

CLASSIC....................*Shake & Strain*
Cocktail glass, chilled
Sugar rim optional
1 oz. Brandy
½ oz. Triple Sec
½ oz. Maraschino Liqueur
1½ oz. sweet 'n' sour
Lemon twist garnish

CLOVER CLUB...........*Shake & Strain*
Cocktail glass, chilled
1½ oz. Gin
½ oz. grenadine
1½ oz. sweet 'n' sour
1 egg white

COBRA
See SLOE SCREW

COCAINE SHOOTER (1)
...........*Shake & Strain*
Rocks or old fashion glass, chilled
¾ oz. Vodka
¾ oz. Chambord
½ oz. Southern Comfort
¾ oz. orange juice
¾ oz. cranberry juice

COCAINE SHOOTER (2)
...........*Shake & Strain*
Rocks or old fashion glass, chilled
1½ oz. Vodka
¾ oz. Chambord
¼ oz. sweet 'n' sour
¼ oz. Seven-up

COCO LOCO..............*Blend with ice*
House specialty glass
1 oz. Gold Tequila
2 oz. coconut cream syrup
3 oz. pineapple juice
Pineapple wedge garnish

COCOMOTION..............*Blend with ice*
House specialty glass, chilled
1½ oz. Myers's Jamaican Rum
2 oz. fresh lime juice
3 oz. coconut syrup
Lime wedge garnish

COFFEE MARNIER FRAPPÉ
See FRAPPÉ, COFFEE MARNIER

COFFEE NUTCAKE......*Blend with ice*
House specialty glass
1½ oz. Kahlua
¾ oz. Frangelico
½ oz. Brown Creme de Cacao
Dash grenadine
2 scoops French vanilla ice cream

COLD FUSION.........*Shake & Strain*
House specialty glass, ice
¾ oz. Stolichnaya Vodka
¾ oz. Midori
½ oz. Triple Sec
½ oz. Rose's lime juice
½ oz. fresh lemon juice
1½ oz. sweet 'n' sour
Lime wedge garnish

COLD GOLD...........*Build*
Highball glass, ice
¾ oz. Orange Schnapps
Fill with orange juice
Float ¾ oz. Blue Curaçao

COLLINS.......*Shake & Strain*
Collins glass, ice
1 oz. requested liquor or liqueur
2 oz. sweet 'n' sour
Shake and strain
Fill with club soda
Orange slice and cherry garnish
 Note: *The following drink names are
 made with the products listed using the
 above recipe:*
TOM COLLINS – Gin
JIM COLLINS – Scotch
JOHN COLLINS – Bourbon
MIKE or **JOE COLLINS** – Irish Whiskey
PEDRO COLLINS – Light Rum
PIERRE COLLINS – Cognac
JACK COLLINS – Applejack

COLORADO AVALANCHE
................***Build*
Coffee mug, heated
½ oz. Kahlua
½ oz. Brown Creme de Cacao
½ oz. Chambord
Fill with hot Nestle's Alpine White Cocoa
*Whipped cream garnishtopped with
 Sprinkle of powdered cocoa*

COLORADO BULLDOG...........*Build*
Bucket glass, ice
1½ oz. Vodka
½ oz. Kahlua
½ fill half & half cream
½ fill cola

COLORADO RIVER COOLER
................***Build*
White wine glass, ice
4 oz. White Zinfandel
1 oz. Midori
Fill with club soda

COMFORTABLE CRUSH...........*Build*
Bucket glass, ice
½ oz. Vodka
½ oz. Chambord
½ oz. Southern Comfort
Fill with lemonade
Lemon wedge garnish

COMFORTABLE SCREW...........*Build*
a.k.a. SOUTHERN SCREW
Highball glass, ice
1 oz. Southern Comfort
Fill with orange juice

COMMODORE...........*Shake & Strain*
Cocktail glass, chilled
2 oz. Amber Rum
½ oz. simple syrup
¾ oz. sweet 'n' sour
2 dashes grenadine
1 egg white

CONCORDE...........*Build*
Champagne glass, chilled
½ oz. Vodka
Fill with Champagne
Float ½ oz. Grand Marnier

CONGO COOLER...........*Build*
Bucket glass, ice
1½ oz. Vodka
Fill with orange juice
Float ½ oz. Creme de Banana

COOKIE....,...........*Build*
Rocks glass, ice
1½ oz. Vodka
½ oz. Kahlua
½ oz. Peppermint Schnapps

COOKIES 'N' CREAM
................***Blend with ice*
House specialty glass
1 oz. Brown Creme de Cacao
1 oz. half & half cream
1–2 scoops ice cream
2-3 Oreo cookies

COOL CAPTAIN...........*Build*
Presentation shot glass, chilled
1 oz. Captain Morgan's Spiced Rum
¾ oz. Peppermint Schnapps
Dash grenadine

CORONATION.........................*Build*
Wine goblet, ice optional
1 oz. Dry Vermouth
1½ oz. Dry Sherry
Dash Maraschino Liqueur
2 dashes Angostura bitters
5 oz. white wine
Fill with club soda

CORPSE REVIVER (1)......*Stir & Strain*
Cocktail glass, chilled
¾ oz. Calvados
¾ oz. V.S. Cognac
½ oz. Sweet Vermouth
Lemon twist garnish

CORPSE REVIVER (2)......*Stir & Strain*
Cocktail glass, chilled
1 oz. Fernet Branca
1 oz. Brandy
1 oz. White Creme de Cacao

COSSACK
See WHITE SPIDER

COYOTE MARGARITA
See MARGARITA, COYOTE

CRAB HOUSE SHOOTER
.............*Shake & strain*
Presentation shot, chilled or rocks glass, ice
½ oz. Amaretto di Saronno
½ oz. Southern Comfort
½ oz. Chambord
¼ oz. sweet 'n' sour
¼ oz. Mauna Lai juice (Ocean Spray)
¼ oz. pineapple juice
¼ oz. cranberry juice
¼ oz. orange juice

CRANBERRY KAMIKAZE
See KAMIKAZE, CRANBERRY

CREAMSICKLE (1)......*Shake or Blend*
Cocktail or house specialty glass, chilled
½ oz. Creme de Banana
½ oz. Triple Sec
1 oz. orange juice
1 oz. half & half cream

CREAMSICKLE (2)......*Blend with ice*
House specialty glass, ice
1¼ oz. Amaretto di Saronno
¾ oz. Triple Sec
2 oz. orange juice
1 scoop vanilla ice cream
1 scoop orange sorbet
Whipped cream garnish

CREAMY BULL............*Shake or Blend*
Cocktail glass, chilled or house specialty glass
½ oz. Tequila
½ oz. Kahlua
2 oz. half & half cream

CRYSTAL CLEAR.........*Shake & Strain*
House specialty glass, ice
1 oz. Vodka
¾ oz. Midori
¾ oz. Peach Schnapps
½ oz. grape juice
1½ oz. cranberry juice
2 oz. orange juice

CRYSTAL KAMI
See KAMIKAZE, CRYSTAL

CUBA LIBRE...........................*Build*
Highball glass, ice
1 oz. Light Rum
Fill with cola
Lime wedge garnish

CUBAN PEACH............*Shake & Strain*
Cocktail glass, chilled
1½ oz. Light Rum
½ oz. Rose's lime juice
Dash simple syrup
Mint sprig garnish

CYRANO......................*Shake & Strain*
Presentation shot glass, chilled
1 oz. Bailey's Irish Cream
1 oz. Grand Marnier
Shake and strain
Splash Chambord

DAIQUIRI..................*Shake or Blend*
Cocktail or house specialty glass, chilled
1 oz. Light Rum
2 oz. sweet 'n' sour
¼ oz. Rose's lime juice optional
Lime wheel garnish

DAIQUIRI, FRUIT.........*Blend with ice*
House specialty glass
1 oz. Light Rum
2 oz. sweet 'n' sour
½ cup requested fruit

DANGEROUS LIAISONS
.............*Shake & Strain*
Sherry glass, chilled
1 oz. Brandy
1 oz. Cointreau
½ oz. sweet 'n' sour

DANISH MARY......................*Build*
Bucket or house specialty glass, ice
Salted rim optional
1¼ oz. Aquavit
Fill with Bloody Mary mix
Lime wedge and celery garnish

DARK & STORMY....................*Build*
Highball glass, ice
1¼ oz. Bacardi Black Label
Fill with Jamaican ginger beer
Lime wedge garnish

DEATH IN THE AFTERNOON
See HEMINGWAY

DEATH OF A VIRGIN............*Build*
Bucket glass, ice
1½ oz. Vodka
1½ oz. Peach Schnapps
½ oz. Rose's lime juice
½ fill orange juice
½ fill Seven-up
Orange slice and cherry garnish

DEATHWISH.......................*Build*
Presentation shot glass, chilled
½ oz. Wild Turkey 101 proof
½ oz. Bacardi Gold Reserve Rum
½ oz. Peppermint Schnapps
½ oz. grenadine

DEAUVILLE............*Shake & Strain*
Cocktail glass, chilled
1¼ oz. Applejack or Calvados
½ oz. Triple Sec
½ oz. grenadine
1½ oz. sweet 'n' sour

DEBUTANT............*Shake & Strain*
Cocktail glass, chilled
½ oz. Tequila
½ oz. Peach Schnapps
½ oz. Cusenier Freezomint
1½ oz. sweet 'n' sour
Lemon twist garnish

DEEP THROAT....................*Build*
Presentation shot glass, chilled
1 oz. Stolichnaya Vodka
1 oz. Tia Maria
Whipped cream garnish

De GAULLE COCKTAIL
..........*Shake & Strain*
Champagne glass, chilled
¾ oz. V.S. Cognac
¾ oz. Chambord
1 oz. sweet 'n' sour
Shake and strain
Fill with Champagne
Lemon wheel garnish

De GAULLE'S DESSERT
............*Blend with ice*
House specialty glass, chilled
1½ oz. Benedictine & Brandy (B & B)
¾ oz. simple syrup
3-4 dashes grenadine
1-2 scoops vanilla ice cream
Shaved chocolate garnish

DELMONICO
See BRANDY MANHATTAN

DEPTHCHARGE
See BOILERMAKER

DESERT SCREW
See CALIFORNIA SCREW

DESERT STORM......*Shake & Strain*
Bucket glass, ice
1 oz. Maui Tropical Schnapps
1 oz. Amaretto di Saronno
½ oz. sweet 'n' sour
1½ oz. pineapple juice
1½ oz. orange juice

DESERT SUNRISE....................*Build*
Bucket glass, ice
1 oz. Tequila
½ oz. Blue Curaçao
Fill with orange juice
Splash sweet 'n' sour

DESIGNER JEANS....................*Build*
Presentation shot glass, chilled
⅓ fill Bailey's Irish Cream
⅓ fill Raspberry Schnapps
⅓ fill Myers's Jamaican Rum

DEVINE WIND
See BLUE KAMIKAZE

DEW DROP DEAD.................*Build*
Mason Jar, ice
2½ oz. Georgia Moonshine Corn Whiskey
½ oz. Triple Sec
Fill with white grape juice

DIABLO......................*Stir & Strain*
Cocktail glass, chilled or rocks glass, ice
1½ oz. Brandy
½ oz. Dry Vermouth
½ oz. Triple Sec
2 dashes Angostura bitters
Cherry or lemon twist garnish

DIKI-DIKI...............*Shake & Strain*
Cocktail glass, chilled
1½ oz. Applejack or Calvados
¾ oz. Gin
1 oz. grapefruit juice

DIRE STRAITS.....................*Build*
a.k.a. DIRTY MOTHER F'ER
Rocks glass, ice
1½ oz. Brandy
½ oz. Kahlua
½ oz. Galliano
½ oz. half & half cream

DIRTY ASHTRAY.........*Shake & Strain*
House specialty glass, ice
½ oz. Gin
½ oz. Vodka
½ oz. Light Rum
½ oz. Tequila
½ oz. Blue Curaçao
½ oz. grenadine
2 oz. sweet 'n' sour
1½ oz. pineapple juice
Lemon wedge garnish

DIRTY BANANA.........*Shake or Blend*
Cocktail glass, chilled or house specialty glass
½ oz. Brown Creme de Cacao
½ oz. Creme de Banana
2 oz. half & half cream

DIRTY HARRY.....................*Build*
Presentation shot glass, chilled
1 oz. Tia Maria
1 oz. Grand Marnier

DIRTY MOTHER.................*Build*
a.k.a. DIRTY WHITE MOTHER
Rocks glass, ice
1½ oz. Brandy
½ oz. Kahlua
½ oz. half & half cream

DOCTOR'S ADVICE
.........*Shake & Strain*
Cocktail glass, chilled
1 oz. Dr. McGillicuddy's Mentholmint
1 oz. Kahlua
1 oz. White Creme de Cacao

DOCTOR'S ELIXIR....................*Build*
Rocks glass, ice
1 oz. Chambord
1 oz. Dr. McGillicuddy's Mentholmint

DONE & BRADSTREET
..............*Stir & Strain*
Cocktail glass, chilled
1 oz. Absolut Vodka
½ oz. Absolut Citron
½ oz. Blue Curaçao
½ oz. Midori
¼ oz. Rose's lime juice
Lime wheel garnish

DOUBLE AGENT......*Shake & Strain*
Bucket glass, ice
1½ oz. Vodka
1 oz. sweet 'n' sour
½ oz. Rose's lime juice
½ oz. grenadine
Shake and strain
Fill with Seven-up

DOWNEASTER....................*Build*
Highball glass, ice
1 oz. Vodka
½ fill cranberry juice
½ fill pineapple juice

DOWN UNDER...........*Shake & Strain*
House specialty glass, ice
1¼ oz. Amaretto di Saronno
2 oz. orange juice
2 oz. sweet 'n' sour
Shake and strain
Fill with Champagne

DOWN UNDER SNOWBALL
............*Blend with ice*
House specialty glass
1 oz. Light Rum
1 oz. Peach Schnapps
1 oz. grenadine
4 oz. orange juice

DRAGOON..........................*Build*
Sherry glass, chilled
⅓ fill Opal Nera Sambuca
⅓ fill Kahlua
⅓ fill Bailey's Irish Cream

DR. PEPPER (1)......................*Build*
a.k.a. EASY RIDER
Highball glass, ice
1 oz. Amaretto di Saronno
Fill with club soda

DR. PEPPER (2)........................*Build*
Beer mug & shot glass, chilled
1 oz. Amaretto di Saronno
7-8 oz. draft beer
   Fill shot glass with Amaretto and drop into beer.

DR. PEPPER FROM HELL.........*Build*
Beer mug and shot glass, chilled
Into shot glass:
½ fill Amaretto di Saronno
½ fill 151 proof Rum
   Ignite rum and drop into ¾ filled glass of draft beer.

DREAMSICKLE (1).................*Build*
Highball glass, ice
1 oz. Amaretto di Saronno
½ fill half & half cream
½ fill orange juice
Float ½ oz. Galliano optional

DREAMSICKLE (2).................*Build*
Bucket glass, ice
1¼ oz. Licor 43
½ fill half & half cream
½ fill orange juice
Orange wheel garnish

DRY ARROYO.........*Shake & Strain*
Champagne glass, chilled
¾ oz. Tia Maria
¾ oz. Chambord
1½ oz. orange juice
¾ oz. sweet 'n' sour
Shake and strain
Fill with Champagne
Orange twist garnish

DRY BRANDY MANHATTAN
See MANHATTAN, DRY BRANDY

DRY MANHATTAN
See MANHATTAN, DRY

DRY MARTINI
See MARTINI, DRY

DRY ROB ROY
See ROB ROY, DRY

DUBONNET COCKTAIL
...............*Stir & Strain*
Cocktail glass, chilled
1½ oz. Gin
1½ oz. Dubonnet
Lemon twist garnish

DUCK FART...........................*Layer*
Presentation shot glass, chilled
⅓ fill Kahlua
⅓ fill Bailey's Irish Cream
⅓ fill Crown Royal

DUKE OF EARL.....................*Build*
Coffee mug, heated
1¼ oz. Kahlua
½ oz. Bacardi Black Label Rum
½ oz. Amaretto di Saronno
1 tbsp. Tom & Jerry batter
Fill with frothed milk
   Note: *See recipe for Tom & Jerry batter*

DUSTY ROSE........................*Build*
Presentation shot glass, chilled
1 oz. Chambord
1 oz. Bailey's Irish Cream

DUTCH COFFEE....................*Build*
Coffee mug, heated
1 oz. Vandermint
Fill with hot coffee
Whipped cream garnish

DUTCH MARTINI
See MARTINI, DUTCH

DUTCH VELVET.........*Shake or Blend*
Cocktail or house specialty glass, chilled
¾ oz. Vandermint
½ oz. Creme de Banana
2 oz. half & half cream
Shaved chocolate garnish

DYING NAZI FROM HELL.........*Build*
Presentation shot glass, chilled
⅓ fill Jägermeister
⅓ fill Bailey's Irish Cream
⅓ fill Stolichnaya Vodka

EARL OF GREY.......................*Build*
Tea or coffee cup, heated
1¼ oz. Scotch
Fill with hot Earl Grey tea
Lemon wedge garnish

EAST INDIA............*Shake & Strain*
Cocktail glass, chilled
1½ oz. Brandy
½ oz. Triple Sec
Dash Angostura bitters
1 oz. pineapple juice
Lemon twist garnish

EASY RIDER
See DR. PEPPER (1)

ECSTACY SHOOTER
.........Shake & Strain
Rocks glass, chilled
1 oz. Chambord
½ oz. Vodka
½ oz. cranberry juice
1 oz. pineapple juice

ED SULLIVAN...............*Blend with ice*
House specialty glass
¾ oz. Light Rum
¾ oz. Amaretto di Saronno
⅓ cup strawberries
½ oz. half & half cream
Blend with ice
Fill with Champagne
Strawberry garnish

ELECTRIC LEMONADE
.........Shake & Strain
House specialty glass
½ oz. Vodka
½ oz. Gin
½ oz. Light Rum
½ oz. Triple Sec
2 oz. sweet 'n' sour
Shake and strain
Fill with Seven-up
   Note: *Substitute Blue Curaçao for Triple Sec*
   to make **ADIOS MOTHER**.

ELECTRIC WATERMELON
.........Shake & Strain
House specialty glass, ice
¾ oz. Midori
½ oz. Vodka
½ oz. Light Rum
½ oz. grenadine
2 oz. orange juice
Shake and strain
Fill with Seven-up

EMBOLISM.............................*Build*
Presentation shot glass, chilled
½ fill Bailey's Irish Cream
½ fill Raspberry Schnapps
   Note: *May also be made using Chambord*
   instead of raspberry schnapps.

EMERALD ICE............*Blend with ice*
House specialty glass
¾ oz. Cinnamon Schnapps
¾ oz. Green Creme de Menthe
1–2 scoops ice cream
1½ oz. half & half cream

EMERALD ISLE........................*Build*
Cappuccino cup, heated
½ oz. Irish Mist
½ oz. Bailey's Irish Cream
¼ oz. Irish whiskey
¼ oz. Kahlua
¾ fill with hot espresso coffee
Spoon on frothed milk
Shaved chocolate garnish

EMPIRE STATE SLAMMER
.........Shake & Strain
Old fashion glass, chilled
¾ oz. Canadian Whisky
¼ oz. Creme de Banana
¼ oz. Sloe Gin
3 oz. orange juice

ENGLISH MULE.....................*Build*
Ale or beer glass, ice
3 oz. Green ginger beer
1½ oz. Gin
2½ oz. orange juice
Fill with club soda
Preserved ginger garnish optional

E PLURIBUS UNUM......*Blend with ice*
House specialty glass
¾ oz. Frangelico
¾ oz. Chambord
¾ oz. Kahlua
2 scoops chocolate ice cream
Shaved white chocolate garnish

ERIE CANAL........................*Build*
Rocks glass, ice
1½ oz. Irish Whiskey
½ oz. Irish Mist
½ oz. Bailey's Irish Cream

E.T. ....*Build*
Presentation shot glass, chilled
⅓ fill Midori
⅓ fill Bailey's Irish Cream
⅓ fill Stolichnaya Vodka

EXPRESS MAIL DROP
............Shake & Strain
Champagne glass, chilled
1¼ oz. Amaretto di Saronno
½ oz. Chambord
2½ oz. orange juice
Shake and strain
Fill with Champagne

EXTRA DRY MARTINI
See **MARTINI, EXTRA DRY**

EXTRA DRY VODKA MARTINI
See MARTINI, EXTRA DRY VODKA

EYE TO EYE...............*Shake & Strain*
Rocks glass, chilled
1 oz. Bailey's Irish Cream
1 oz. Irish Whiskey

F-16................................*Build*
a.k.a. CARMALITA
Presentation shot glass, chilled
⅓ fill Kahlua
⅓ fill Bailey's Irish Cream
⅓ fill Frangelico

FACE ERASER........................*Build*
Old fashion glass, crushed ice
1 oz. Vodka
1 oz. Kahlua
Fill with Seven-up

FAHRENHEIT 5000...............*Build*
Presentation shot glass
Cover bottom of glass with Tabasco sauce
1 oz. Cinnamon Schnapps
1 oz. Absolut Peppar

FEDERAL EXPRESS......*Shake & Strain*
Champagne glass, chilled
1¼ oz. Amaretto di Saronno
½ oz. Chambord
2½ oz. sweet 'n' sour
Shake and strain
Fill with Champagne
Lemon twist garnish

FEDORA.................*Shake & Strain*
Cocktail glass, chilled
¾ oz. Brandy
¾ oz. Bourbon or Rye Whiskey
¾ oz. Myers's Jamaican Rum
½ oz. Triple Sec
1 oz. sweet 'n' sour

FIDEL'S MARTINI
See MARTINI, FIDEL'S

'57 T-BIRD WITH
** FLORIDA PLATES**
.......................*Build*
Highball glass, ice
½ oz. Stolichnaya Vodka
½ oz. Amaretto di Saronno
½ oz. Grand Marnier
Fill with orange juice

'57 T-BIRD WITH
** HAWAIIAN PLATES**
.......................*Build*
Highball glass, ice
½ oz. Stolichnaya Vodka
½ oz. Amaretto di Saronno
½ oz. Grand Marnier
Fill with pineapple juice

FIREBALL............................*Build*
a.k.a. JAW BREAKER
Presentation shot glass
Fill with Cinnamon Schnapps
Dash Tabasco sauce

FIRECRACKER..........................*Build*
Collins glass, ice
1½ oz. Captain Morgan's Spiced Rum
½ oz. grenadine
Fill with orange juice
Float ½ oz. 151 Rum

FIRE IN THE HOLE.................*Build*
Presentation shot glass
1½ oz. Ouzo
2-3 dashes Tabasco sauce

FIRE 'N' ICE...............*Blend with ice*
House specialty glass
¾ oz. Cinnamon Schnapps
¾ oz. White Creme de Cacao
1½ oz. half & half cream
1–2 scoops ice cream

FLAMING ARMADILLO
............*Stir & Strain*
Presentation shot glass, chilled
¾ oz. Kahlua
¾ oz. Amaretto di Saronno
¾ oz. Grand Marnier
¾ oz. Bacardi Black Label Rum

FLAMING BLUE JEANS
........*Shake & Strain*
a.k.a. FLAMING BLUE JESUS
Rocks glass, ice
1 oz. Southern Comfort
¾ oz. Peppermint Schnapps
¾ oz. Blackberry Schnapps
¼ oz. 151 Rum

FLAMINGO..........................*Build*
Bucket glass, ice
1½ oz. Light Rum
¾ oz. grenadine
½ fill orange juice
½ fill sweet 'n' sour

FLORIDA...............*Shake & Strain*
Collins glass, ice
1½ oz. Light Rum
½ oz. Green Creme de Menthe
½ oz. Rose's lime juice
½ oz. pineapple juice
Dash simple syrup
Shake and strain
Fill with club soda
Mint sprig garnish

FLORIDA ICED TEA
See ICED TEA, FLORIDA

FLORIDA T-BACK
.........*Shake & Strain*
Bucket glass, ice
1 oz. Myers's Jamaican Rum
1 oz. Malibu Rum
½ oz. grenadine
1½ oz. pineapple juice
1½ oz. orange juice
Pineapple wedge and cherry garnish

FLYING KANGAROO
See PIÑA COLADA, AUSSIE

FOGCUTTER............*Shake & Strain*
Collins glass, ice
½ oz. Brandy
½ oz. Light Rum
½ oz. Gin
1½ oz. sweet 'n' sour
1½ oz. orange juice
Shake and strain
Float ½ oz. Sherry

FOREIGN LEGION...............*Build*
Cappuccino cup, heated
½ oz. Brandy
½ oz. Benedictine D.O.M.
½ oz. Frangelico
½ oz. Amaretto di Saronno
¾ fill with espresso coffee
Spoon on frothed milk
Shaved chocolate garnish

FOREVER AMBER.................*Build*
Brandy snifter, heated
1½ oz. Tuaca
½ oz. Brandy

.44 MAGNUM.........*Shake & Strain*
Collins glass, ice
½ oz. Bacardi Light Rum
½ oz. Bacardi Black Label Rum
½ oz. Myers's Jamaican Rum
½ oz. Vodka
½ oz. Triple Sec
½ oz. pineapple juice
1½ oz. sweet 'n' sour
Shake and strain
Fill with 7-up

FOUR-WAY POUSSE CAFÉ
See POUSSE CAFÉ, FOUR-WAY

FRANGELICO FREEZE
............*Blend with ice*
House specialty glass
½ oz. Frangelico
½ oz. Chocolate Schnapps
½ oz. Kahlua
1–2 scoops vanilla ice cream

FRAPPÉ................................*Build*
Cocktail or Champagne saucer, chilled
Fill with crushed ice
1½ oz. requested liqueur
Pour over mounded ice
Short straw

FRAPPÉ, APRICOT BRANDY......*Build*
Cocktail or Champagne saucer, chilled
Fill with crushed ice
¾ oz. Brandy
½ oz. Apricot Brandy
¼ oz. Creme de Noyaux
Short straw

FRAPPÉ, BANANA RUM.........*Build*
Cocktail or Champagne saucer, chilled
Fill with crushed ice
½ oz. Creme de Banana
½ oz. Light Rum
½ oz. orange juice
Short straw

FRAPPÉ, COFFEE MARNIER
....................*Build*
Cocktail or Champagne saucer, chilled
Fill with crushed ice
¾ oz. Kahlua
¾ oz. Grand Marnier
Splash orange juice
Short straw

FRAPPÉ, LEMON.................*Build*
Cocktail or Champagne saucer, chilled
Fill with crushed ice
¾ oz. Tuaca
¾ oz. sweet 'n' sour
Short straw

FRAPPÉ, MOCHA..................*Build*
Cocktail or Champagne saucer, chilled
Fill with crushed ice
¾ oz. Kahlua
¼ oz. White Creme de Menthe
¼ oz. White Creme de Cacao
¼ oz. Triple Sec
Short straw

FRAPPÉ, PARISIAN...............*Build*
Cocktail or Champagne saucer, chilled
Fill with crushed ice
¾ oz. Yellow Chartreuse
¾ oz. V.S. Cognac
Short straw

FRAPPÉ, SAMBUCA MOCHA
......................*Build*
Cocktail or Champagne saucer, chilled
Fill with crushed ice
¾ oz. Kahlua
¾ oz. Sambuca
3 roasted coffee beans
Short straw

FREDDY FUDPUCKER............*Build*
**a.k.a. CHARLIE GOODLEG,
CACTUS BANGER**
Bucket glass, ice
1 oz. Tequila
Fill with orange juice
Float ½ oz. Galliano

FREDDY KRUGER.................*Layer*
Presentation shot glass, chilled
⅓ fill Sambuca
⅓ fill Jägermeister
⅓ fill Stolichnaya Vodka

FRENCH CONNECTION.........*Build*
Brandy snifter, heated
¾ oz. V.S. Cognac
¾ oz. Grand Marnier

FRENCH CONSULATE
.........*Shake & Strain*
House specialty glass, chilled
¾ oz. Benedictine D.O.M.
¾ oz. Brandy
½ oz. Cointreau
2 oz. sweet 'n' sour
½ oz. orange juice
Shake and strain
Fill with Champagne
Lemon twist garnish

FRENCH DREAM....................*Build*
Brandy snifter, ice
1 oz. Bailey's Irish Cream
¾ oz. Chambord
¾ oz. Tia Maria

FRENCH KAMIKAZE
See KAMIKAZE, FRENCH

FRENCH KISS........................*Build*
Coffee mug, heated
¾ oz. Kahlua
¾ oz. Amaretto di Saronno
Fill with hot cocoa
Whipped cream garnish

FRENCH MAID'S CAFÉ........*Build*
Coffee mug, heated
½ oz. Kahlua
½ oz. Grand Marnier
½ oz. Brandy
Fill with hot coffee
Whipped cream garnish

FRENCH MANDARINE.........*Build*
Brandy snifter, heated
1½ oz. Armagnac
½ oz. Mandarine Napoleon

FRENCH MARTINI
See MARTINI, FRENCH

FRENCH 75 (1)...........*Shake & Strain*
Champagne glass, chilled
1 oz. Gin
2 oz. sweet 'n' sour
Shake and strain
Fill with Champagne
Lemon twist garnish

FRENCH 75 (2)........*Shake & Strain*
a.k.a. FRENCH 125
Champagne glass, chilled
1 oz. V.S. Cognac
2 oz. sweet 'n' sour
Shake and strain
Fill with Champagne
Lemon twist garnish

FRENCH 95...............*Shake & Strain*
Champagne glass, chilled
1 oz. Bourbon
2 oz. sweet 'n' sour
Shake and strain
Fill with Champagne
Lemon twist garnish

FRENCH 125
See FRENCH 75 (2)

FREUDIAN SLIP........*Shake & Strain*
Champagne glass, chilled
1 oz. Brandy
¾ oz. Grand Marnier
1½ oz. sweet 'n' sour
Shake and strain
Fill with Champagne
Orange twist garnish

FROSTBITE...............*Blend with ice*
House specialty glass, chilled
1½ oz. Yukon Jack
¾ oz. Peppermint Schnapps
2½ oz. sweet 'n' sour

FROSTED PEACH BREEZE
.........*Blend with ice*
House specialty glass, chilled
1 oz. Peach Schnapps
¾ oz. Vodka
2 oz. cranberry juice
2 oz. grapefruit juice

FROSTY NAVEL.........*Blend with ice*
House specialty glass, chilled
1 oz. Peach Schnapps
1½ oz. orange juice
1½ oz. half & half cream
1–2 scoops vanilla ice cream

FROZEN MONK.........*Blend with ice*
House specialty glass, chilled
¾ oz. Frangelico
¾ oz. Kahlua
¾ oz. Brown Creme de Cacao
1–2 scoops vanilla ice cream

FULL MOON........................*Build*
Brandy snifter, heated
¾ oz. Grand Marnier
¾ oz. Amaretto di Saronno

FU MANCHU............*Stir & Strain*
Cocktail glass, chilled
1½ oz. Dark Rum
½ oz. Triple Sec
½ oz. White Creme de Menthe
½ oz. Rose's lime juice
Dash simple syrup
Orange twist garnish

FUZZY DICK........................*Build*
Coffee mug, heated
¾ oz. Grand Marnier
¾ oz. Kahlua
Fill with hot coffee
Whipped cream garnish

FUZZY NAVEL.....................*Build*
a.k.a. PEACH FUZZ
Highball glass, ice
1 oz. Peach Schnapps
Fill with orange juice

GALLIANO STINGER............*Build*
Rocks glass, ice
1½ oz. Galliano
½ oz. White Creme de Menthe

GANG GREEN...........*Shake & Strain*
Bucket glass, ice
1 oz. Light Rum
1 oz. Midori
½ oz. Captain Morgan's Spiced Rum
½ oz. Blue Curaçao
4 oz. sweet 'n' sour

GATOR JUICE.....................*Build*
Bucket glass, ice
1¼ oz. Crystal Comfort
¼ oz. Rose's lime juice
Fill with orange juice
Float ½ oz. Blue Curaçao

GENTLEMAN'S BOILERMAKER
.....................*Build*
Brandy snifter, heated
1 oz. Armagnac
1 oz. Tawny Port

GEORGIA MARGARITA
See MARGARITA, GEORGIA

GEORGIA PEACH..............*Build*
Highball glass, ice
1 oz. Peach Schnapps
Fill with cranberry juice

GEORGIA TURNOVER.........*Build*
Coffee mug, heated
1½ oz. Peach Schnapps
1½ oz. cranberry juice
Fill with hot apple cider

GERMAN CHOCOLATE CAKE
............*Shake or Blend*
Cocktail or house specialty glass, chilled
½ oz. Bailey's Irish Cream
½ oz. Kahlua
½ oz. Frangelico
1½ oz. half & half cream

GIBSON.....................*Build or Stir*
Cocktail glass, chilled or rocks glass, ice
5-8 drops Dry Vermouth
1½ oz. Gin
Cocktail onion garnish
  Note: *GIBSON is a MARTINI garnished with cocktail onions instead of green olives.*

GIBSON, DRY............*Build or Stir*
Cocktail glass, chilled or rocks glass, ice
3-4 drops Dry Vermouth
1½ oz. Gin
Cocktail onion garnish
  Note: *Use little or no dry vermouth to make an* **EXTRA DRY GIBSON**

GIBSON, VODKA.........*Build or Stir*
Cocktail glass, chilled or rocks glass, ice
5-8 drops Dry Vermouth
1½ oz. Vodka
Cocktail onion garnish

GIBSON, VODKA DRY
.............*Build or Stir*
Cocktail glass, chilled or rocks glass, ice
3-4 drops Dry Vermouth
1½ oz. Gin
Cocktail onion garnish
   Note: *Use little or no dry vermouth to make*
an **EXTRA DRY VODKA GIBSON**

GIMLET.....................*Build or Stir*
Cocktail glass, chilled or rocks glass, ice
1½ oz. Gin
½ oz. Rose's lime juice
Lime wedge garnish

GIMLET, RASPBERRY......*Build or Stir*
Cocktail glass, chilled or rocks glass, ice
1½ oz. raspberry-steeped vodka
½ oz. fresh lime juice
½ oz. Rose's lime juice
Lime wedge garnish

GIMLET, TUACA.........*Build or Stir*
Cocktail glass, chilled or rocks glass, ice
1½ oz. Vodka
¾ oz. Tuaca
½ oz. Rose's lime juice
Lime wedge garnish

GIMLET, VODKA.........*Build or Stir*
Cocktail glass, chilled or rocks glass, ice
1½ oz. Vodka
½ oz. Rose's lime juice
Lime wedge garnish

GIN ALEXANDER......*Shake or Blend*
a.k.a. PLAIN ALEXANDER
Cocktail or house specialty glass, chilled
¾ oz. Gin
¾ oz. White Creme de Cacao
2 oz. half & half cream
Nutmeg garnish

GIN FIZZ
See TOM COLLINS

GIN MARY
See BLOODY MARY, GIN

GIN RICKEY........................*Build*
Highball glass, ice
1 oz. Gin
Fill with club soda
Lime wedge garnish

GIRL SCOUT COOKIE
.........*Shake or Blend*
Cocktail or house specialty glass, chilled
¾ oz. Peppermint Schnapps
¾ oz. Kahlua
1½ oz. half & half cream
Cookie garnish

GLACIER BREEZE...............*Build*
Bucket glass, ice
1½ oz. Vodka
¾ fill orange juice
Splash cranberry juice
Splash apple juice

GLASS TOWER.....................*Build*
House specialty glass, ice
1 oz. Vodka
1 oz. Peach Schnapps
1 oz. Bacardi Light Rum
1 oz. Triple Sec
½ oz. Sambuca
Fill with Seven-up

GLASTNOST............*Shake & Strain*
Bucket glass, ice
1 oz. Stolichnaya Vodka
1 oz. Chambord
2 oz. sweet 'n' sour
2 oz. orange juice
Orange slice and cherry garnish

GLOOMCHASER.........*Shake & Strain*
Cocktail glass, chilled
1 oz. Grand Marnier
1 oz. Cointreau
1 oz. sweet 'n' sour
½ oz. grenadine

GLOOMRAISER............*Stir & Strain*
Cocktail glass, chilled
1½ oz. Gin
¼ oz. Dry Vermouth
2 dashes Pernod
2 dashes grenadine
Cherry garnish optional

GOAL POST........................*Layer*
Presentation shot glass
½ fill White Creme de Menthe
½ fill Tequila

GODCHILD..........................*Build*
Rocks glass, ice
1½ oz. Vodka
½ oz. Amaretto di Saronno
½ oz. half & half cream

GODFATHER......................*Build*
Rocks glass, ice
1½ oz. Scotch
½ oz. Amaretto di Saronno

GODMOTHER......................*Build*
Rocks glass, ice
1½ oz. Vodka
½ oz. Amaretto di Saronno

GOLDEN CADILLAC
.........*Shake or Blend*
Cocktail or house specialty glass, chilled
¾ oz. White Creme de Cacao
¾ oz. Galliano
2 oz. half & half cream

GOLDEN DREAM......*Shake or Blend*
Cocktail or house specialty glass, chilled
½ oz. Galliano
½ oz. Triple Sec
½ oz. orange juice
1½ oz. half & half cream

GOLDEN DREAM
WITH DOUBLE BUMPERS
.........*Shake or Blend*
Cocktail or house specialty glass, chilled
½ oz. Galliano
½ oz. Triple Sec
½ oz. Brandy
½ oz. Benedictine D.O.M.
½ oz. orange juice
1½ oz. half & half cream

GOLDEN FIZZ.........*Shake & Strain*
Collins glass, ice
1 oz. Gin
½ oz. simple syrup
1½ oz. sweet 'n' sour
1½ oz. half & half cream
1 egg yolk
Shake and strain
Splash club soda

GOLDEN MAX......................*Build*
Brandy snifter, heated
1½ oz. V.S. Cognac
½ oz. Cointreau

GOLDEN NAIL......................*Build*
Highball glass, ice
1 oz. Drambuie
Fill with grapefruit juice

GOLDEN RAM...........*Blend with ice*
House specialty glass, chilled
1 oz. Southern Comfort
½ oz. Galliano
½ oz. Amaretto di Saronno
½ oz. Peach Schnapps
3 oz. orange juice

GOLDEN SCREW..................*Build*
a.k.a. ITALIAN SCREW
Highball glass, ice
1 oz. Galliano
Fill with orange juice

GOLD MARGARITA
See MARGARITA, GOLD

GOLD RUSH...............*Stir & Strain*
Cocktail glass, chilled or rocks glass, ice
Salted rim optional
1½ oz. Cuervo Especial Tequila
½ oz. Grand Marnier
½ oz. Rose's lime juice
Lime wedge garnish

GOOD & PLENTY..................*Build*
Rocks glass, ice
1½ oz. Kahlua
½ oz. Anisette

GRAND ALLIANCE...............*Build*
Sherry glass, chilled
½ fill Amaretto di Saronno
½ fill Champagne

GRAND SIDE CAR......*Shake & Strain*
Cocktail glass, chilled or brandy snifter, ice
1¼ oz. Brandy
¾ oz. Grand Marnier
1½ oz. sweet 'n' sour

GRASSHOPPER.........*Shake or Blend*
Cocktail or house specialty glass, chilled
¾ oz. White Creme de Cacao
¾ oz. Green Creme de Menthe
2 oz. half & half cream

GREEK COFFEE....................*Build*
Coffee mug, heated
¾ oz. Metaxa 5 Star Brandy
¾ oz. Ouzo
Fill with hot coffee

GREEN EYES
See MIDORI PIÑA COLADA

GREEN HORNET..................*Build*
a.k.a. IRISH STINGER
Rocks glass, ice
1½ oz. Brandy
½ oz. Green Creme de Menthe

GREEN IGUANA
See MARGARITA, MELON

GREEN LIZARD.....................*Layer*
Presentation shot glass
½ fill Green Chartreuse
½ fill 151 Rum

GREEN RUSSIAN.................*Build*
Rocks glass, ice
1½ oz. Vodka
½ oz. Midori

GREEN SNEAKERS......*Shake & Strain*
Old fashion glass, chilled
1 oz. Vodka
½ oz. Midori
½ oz. Triple Sec
2 oz. orange juice

GREEN SPIDER.....................*Build*
Rocks glass, ice
1½ oz. Vodka
½ oz. Green Creme de Menthe

GREYHOUND.......................*Build*
Highball glass, ice
1 oz. Vodka
Fill with grapefruit juice
Note: *May be requested made with Gin*

GUAVA COOLER......*Shake & Strain*
Collins glass, ice
1½ oz. Light Rum
½ oz. Maraschino Liqueur
1½ oz. guava nectar
½ oz. simple syrup
1 oz. sweet 'n' sour
1 oz. pineapple juice

GUAYMUS MARGARITA
See MARGARITA, GUAYMUS

GULF BREEZE.......................*Build*
Highball glass, ice
1 oz. Gin
Splash grapefruit juice
Splash cranberry juice

GULF TIDE...........................*Build*
Highball glass, ice
1 oz. Gin
½ fill orange juice
½ fill cranberry juice

GULLET PLEASER.................*Build*
Presentation shot glass, chilled
⅓ fill Peach Schnapps
⅓ fill Stolichnaya Limonnaya
Splash cranberry juice
Splash grapefruit juice

GUMBY...................*Shake & Strain*
Cocktail glass, chilled
1¼ oz, Vodka
¾ oz. Midori
¾ oz. sweet 'n' sour
Shake and strain
Fill with Seven-up
Cherry garnish

GYPSY........................*Build or Stir*
Cocktail glass, chilled or rocks glass, ice
1½ oz. Vodka
½ oz. Benedictine D.O.M.
Dash Angostura bitters
Lemon twist garnish

HALEKULANI SUNSET
.........*Shake & Strain*
House specialty glass, ice
1½ oz. Light Rum
½ oz. Triple Sec
½ oz. grenadine
3 oz. guava nectar
1½ oz. sweet 'n' sour
Pineapple wedge garnish

HALF & HALF...............*Build or Stir*
Cocktail glass, chilled or rocks glass, ice
1 oz. Dry Vermouth
1 oz. Sweet Vermouth
Lemon twist garnish

HAPPY JACK...........................*Build*
Presentation shot glass
½ fill Jack Daniel's
½ fill Apple Schnapps

HARBOR LIGHTS.................*Layer*
Presentation shot glass
⅓ fill Kahlua
⅓ fill Tequila
⅓ fill 151 proof Rum

HARVARD.................*Build or Stir*
Cocktail glass, chilled or rocks glass, ice
1½ oz. Brandy
½ oz. Sweet Vermouth
2 dashes Angostura bitters
Dash simple syrup
Lemon twist garnish

HARVEST GROG...................*Build*
Coffee mug, heated
1 oz. Laird's Applejack
1 oz. Chambord
6 oz. apple cider
2 dashes cinnamon
3 whole cloves
Cinnamon stick garnish
Heat apple cider and spices in small sauce pan for 5 minutes. Remove cloves; pour mixture into mug with Laird's and Chambord.

HARVEY WALLBANGER......*Build*
Bucket glass, ice
1 oz. Vodka
Fill with orange juice
Float ½ oz. Galliano

HASTA LA VISTA, BABY
.........*Shake & Strain*
Rocks glass, chilled
½ oz. Cuervo Especial Tequila
½ oz. Absolut Peppar
½ oz. Peach Schnapps
Dash Dry Vermouth
1-2 dashes Rose's lime juice
¼ oz. Triple Sec
¼ oz. Creme de Noyaux
¼ oz. B. & B.
¾ oz. pineapple juice
¾ oz. orange juice

HAVANA...............*Shake & Strain*
Cocktail glass, chilled
½ oz. Sherry
1 oz. Amber Rum
1½ oz. sweet 'n' sour
Orange twist garnish

HAVANA CLUB.........*Build or Stir*
Cocktail glass, chilled or rocks glass, ice
½ oz. Sweet Vermouth
1½ oz. Amber Rum
Dash Angostura bitters
Cherry garnish

HAWAIIAN HURRICANE
......*Shake & Strain*
House specialty glass, ice
½ oz. Bacardi Light Rum
½ oz. Bacardi Dark Rum
½ oz. Myers's Jamaican Rum
½ oz. Tequila
½ oz. Vodka
2 oz. pineapple juice
2 oz. papaya juice
Shake and strain
Float ½ oz. 151 Rum
Orange slice and cherry garnish

HAWAIIAN ICED TEA
See ICED TEA, HAWAIIAN

HAWAIIAN PUNCH (1)
.........*Shake & Strain*
Collins glass, ice
1 oz. Vodka
½ oz. Amaretto di Saronno
½ oz. Southern Comfort
½ oz. Sloe Gin
Fill with pineapple juice
Shake and strain
Splash Seven-up optional

HAWAIIAN PUNCH (2).........*Build*
Bucket glass, ice
¾ oz. Southern Comfort
¾ oz. Amaretto di Saronno
¾ oz. Creme de Noyaux
1½ oz. pineapple juice
1½ oz. orange juice

HAWAIIAN SHOOTER
......*Shake & Strain*
Rocks glass, chilled
1¼ oz. Southern Comfort
¾ oz. Creme de Noyaux
¼ oz. pineapple juice

HEARTBREAK......................*Build*
Bucket glass, ice
1¼ oz. Seagram's V.O.
Fill with cranberry juice
Float ½ oz. Brandy

HEATWAVE..........................*Build*
Bucket glass, ice
1 oz. Myers's Jamaican Rum
½ oz. Peach Schnapps
Fill with pineapple juice
Float ½ oz. grenadine

HELENE............................*Build*
Brandy snifter, ice optional
1½ oz. Poire William
½ oz. Chocolate liqueur

HEMINGWAY.....................*Build*
a.k.a. DEATH IN THE AFTERNOON
Champagne glass, chilled
1½ oz. Pernod
Fill with Champagne

HIGHBALL..........................*Build*
Highball glass, ice
1 oz. Bourbon
Fill with ginger ale

HIGHLAND COCKTAIL
............*Stir & Strain*
a.k.a. HIGHLAND FLING
Cocktail glass, chilled or rocks glass, ice
1½ oz. Scotch
½ oz. Sweet Vermouth
Dash Angostura bitters

HOLLYWOOD.....................*Build*
Highball glass, ice
¾ oz. Vodka
¾ oz. Chambord
Fill with pineapple juice

HONEY BEE............*Shake & Strain*
Cocktail glass, chilled
1 oz. Myers's Jamaican Rum
1½ oz. sweet 'n' sour
½ oz. honey

HONEYDEW............*Shake & Strain*
Collins glass, ice
1½ oz. Midori
3 oz. lemonade
Shake and strain
Fill with Champagne

HONEYMOON.........*Shake & Strain*
a.k.a. FARMER'S DAUGHTER
Cocktail glass, chilled
½ oz. Benedictine D.O.M.
½ oz. Triple Sec
1¼ oz. Applejack
1 oz. sweet 'n' sour

HORNY MARGARITA
See MARGARITA, HORNY

HORSE'S NECK WITH A KICK
.....................*Build*
Highball glass, ice
1 oz. Bourbon
Fill with ginger ale
Garnish with long spiral of lemon peel
(a "horse's neck")

HOT APPLE PIE.....................*Build*
Coffee mug, heated
1 oz. Tuaca
Fill with hot apple cider
Whipped cream garnish

HOT BUTTERED RUM............*Build*
Coffee mug, heated
1½ oz. Myers's Jamaican Rum
½ oz. simple syrup
2 pinches nutmeg
Cinnamon stick
Fill with hot water
Float pat of butter

HOT CHAMBORD DREAM......*Build*
Coffee mug, heated
¾ oz. Brown Creme de Cacao
¾ oz. Chambord
4-5 oz. frothed milk

HOT MARTINI
See MARTINI, HOT

HOT MILK PUNCH...............*Build*
Coffee mug, heated
1½ oz. Bourbon
½ oz. simple syrup
Fill with hot milk
Nutmeg garnish

HOT MULLED WINE
......*Build & Simmer*
(Makes 8–10 servings)
Punch bowl or decanter
36 oz. dry red wine
½ oz. cup sugar
12 oz. cranberry juice
¼ cup mulling spices
Heat wine, sugar, juice & spices together and simmer for 30 minutes.

HOT TIMES...........................*Build*
Presentation shot glass
¼ fill Apple Schnapps
¼ fill Cinnamon Schnapps
¼ fill Light Rum
¼ fill hot apple cider

HOT TODDY........................*Build*
Coffee mug, heated
1½ oz. Brandy or Bourbon
1 tsp. sugar
Fill with hot water
Lemon twist garnish

HOUNDSTOOTH.................*Build*
Rocks glass, ice
1½ oz. Vodka
½ oz. White Creme de Cacao
½ oz. Blackberry Brandy

HUMMER.................*Blend with ice*
House specialty glass
¾ oz. Kahlua
¾ oz. Rum
¾ oz. Brown Creme de Cacao
1–2 scoops vanilla ice cream

HUNTER'S COFFEE...............*Build*
Coffee mug, heated
¾ oz. Tia Maria
¾ oz. Cointreau
Fill with hot coffee
Whipped cream garnish topped with ½ oz. Tia Maria

HURRICANE............*Shake & Strain*
House specialty glass, ice
1½ oz. Light Rum
1½ oz. Myers's Jamaican Rum
½ oz. Rose's lime juice
2 dashes simple syrup
½ oz. grenadine
2 oz. orange juice
2 oz. pineapple juice
Fresh fruit garnish

IACOCCA............*Build*
Cappuccino cup, heated
¾ oz. Kahlua
½ oz. Grand Marnier
½ oz. Bailey's Irish Cream
Fill with hot espresso coffee
Froth 3–4 oz. milk mixed
with 1 oz. Frangelico
Spoon on frothed milk
Shaved chocolate garnish

ICEBERG (1)............*Build*
Rocks glass, ice
1½ oz. Vodka
½ oz. Peppermint Schnapps

ICEBERG (2)............*Build*
Rocks glass, ice
1½ oz. Vodka
½ oz. Pernod

ICED TEA, ALASKAN
............*Shake & Strain*
House specialty glass, ice
½ oz. Gin
½ oz. Vodka
½ oz. Light Rum
½ oz. Blue Curaçao
4 oz. sweet 'n' sour
Shake and strain
Fill with Seven-up
Lemon wedge garnish

ICED TEA, BIMINI......*Shake & Strain*
House specialty glass, ice
½ oz. Gin
½ oz. Vodka
½ oz. Light Rum
½ oz. Tequila
½ oz. Blue Curaçao
2 oz. orange juice
2 oz. pineapple juice
1½ oz. sweet 'n' sour
2 oz. cola
Lemon wedge garnish

ICED TEA, CALIFORNIA
............*Shake & Strain*
House specialty glass, ice
½ oz. Gin
½ oz. Vodka
½ oz. Light Rum
½ oz. Tequila
½ oz. Triple Sec
2 oz. sweet 'n' sour
2 oz. grapefruit juice
2 oz. cola
Lemon wedge garnish

ICED TEA, FLORIDA
............*Shake & Strain*
House specialty glass, ice
½ oz. Gin
½ oz. Vodka
½ oz. Light Rum
½ oz. Tequila
½ oz. Triple Sec
2 oz. sweet 'n' sour
2 oz. orange juice
2 oz. cola
Lemon wedge garnish

ICED TEA, HAWAIIAN
............*Shake & Strain*
House specialty glass, ice
½ oz. Gin
½ oz. Vodka
½ oz. Light Rum
½ oz. Tequila
½ oz. Triple Sec
2 oz. sweet 'n' sour
2 oz. pineapple juice
2 oz. cola
Lemon wedge garnish

ICED TEA, LONG BEACH
............*Shake & Strain*
House specialty glass, ice
½ oz. Gin
½ oz. Vodka
½ oz. Light Rum
½ oz. Tequila
½ oz. Triple Sec
2 oz. sweet 'n' sour
2 oz. cranberry juice
2 oz. cola
Lemon wedge garnish

ICED TEA, LONG ISLAND
.........*Shake & Strain*
a.k.a. TEXAS ICED TEA
House specialty glass, ice
½ oz. Gin
½ oz. Vodka
½ oz. Light Rum
½ oz. Tequila
½ oz. Triple Sec
2 oz. sweet 'n' sour
2 oz. cola
Lemon wedge garnish

ICED TEA, RASPBERRY
.........*Shake & Strain*
a.k.a. PURPLE HAZE
House specialty glass, ice
½ oz. Gin
½ oz. Vodka
½ oz. Light Rum
½ oz. Tequila
½ oz. Triple Sec
2 oz. sweet 'n' sour
2 oz. cola
Shake and strain
Float ¾ oz. Chambord
Lemon wedge garnish

ICED TEA, TERMINAL
.........*Shake & Strain*
a.k.a. TERMINAL TEA
House specialty glass, ice
½ oz. Cuervo Especial Tequila
½ oz. Smirnoff Vodka
½ oz. Tanqueray Gin
½ oz. Bacardi Rum
½ oz. Grand Marnier
2 oz. sweet 'n' sour
2 oz. cola
Lemon wedge garnish

ICE PICK.............................*Build*
Collins glass, ice
1¼ oz. Vodka
Fill with lemon-flavored iced tea
Lemon wedge garnish

IDEAL COCKTAIL......*Shake & Strain*
Cocktail glass, chilled
1½ oz. Gin
½ oz. Dry Vermouth
1 oz. grapefruit juice
Dash simple syrup

IL DUCE.....................*Blend with ice*
House specialty glass, chilled
Cinnamon-sugar rim optional
½ oz. Bailey's Irish Cream
½ oz. Frangelico
½ oz. Kahlua
1-2 scoops vanilla ice cream
6 oz. cappuccino (espresso & frothed milk)
Splash half & half cream

INDEPENDENCE SWIZZLE......*Build*
Collins glass, crushed ice
1½ oz. Myers's Jamaican Rum
3 dashes Angostura bitters
¼ oz. honey
½ oz. fresh lime juice
½ oz. simple syrup
  Swizzle thoroughly with bar spoon until glass frosts
Lime wedge garnish

INOCULATION.....................*Layer*
Presentation shot glass, chilled
¾ fill Dr. McGillucuddy's Mentholmint
¼ fill Brandy

INSANE HUSSEIN......*Shake & Strain*
Presentation shot glass, chilled
½ oz. Vodka
½ oz. Galliano
½ oz. Apple Schnapps
½ oz. grapefruit juice

INTERNATIONAL CAPPUCCINO
.......................*Build*
Cappuccino cup, heated
½ oz. Kahlua
½ oz. Amaretto di Saronno
½ oz. Vandermint
½ oz. Myers's Rum Cream
Fill with hot espresso coffee
Spoon on frothed milk
Shaved chocolate garnish

INTERNATIONAL STINGER
.....................*Build*
Rocks glass, ice
1½ oz. Metaxa 5 Star Brandy
½ oz. Galliano

INVERTED NAIL..................*Layer*
Sherry glass
½ fill Drambuie
½ fill Glenfiddich Single Malt

IRANIAN QUAALUDE
See QUAALUDE, IRANIAN

IRISH ALEXANDER
.........*Shake or Blend*
House specialty glass, chilled
1 oz. Irish Mist
¾ oz. White Creme de Cacao
2 oz. half & half cream
Nutmeg garnish

IRISH BROGUE.....................*Build*
Rocks glass, ice
1½ oz. Irish Whiskey
½ oz. Irish Mist

IRISH COFFEE....................*Build*
Coffee mug, heated
1 oz. Irish Whiskey
½ oz. simple syrup
Fill with hot coffee
Top with frothed milk or whipped cream

IRISH COFFEE ROYALE (1)......*Build*
Coffee mug, heated
1 oz. Irish Whiskey
1 oz. Kahlua
½ oz. simple syrup
Fill with hot coffee
Top with frothed milk or whipped cream

IRISH COFFEE ROYALE (2)......Build
Coffee mug, heated
1 oz. Irish Whiskey
¾ oz. Bailey's Irish Cream
½ oz. Irish Mist
Fill with hot coffee
Top with frothed milk or whipped cream

IRISH FLOAT............*Blend with ice*
Beer mug, chilled
1 oz. Bailey's Irish Cream
1 oz. Root Beer Schnapps
1-2 scoops vanilla ice cream
Blend with ice
Fill with root beer

IRISH HEADLOCK......*Shake & Strain*
Presentation shot glass, chilled
½ oz. Bailey's Irish Cream
½ oz. Irish Whiskey
½ oz. Amaretto di saronno
½ oz. Brandy

IRISH MARIA.......................*Build*
Rocks glass, ice
1 oz. Tia Maria
1 oz. Bailey's Irish Cream

IRISH STINGER (1)
See GREEN HORNET

IRISH STINGER (2)..............*Build*
Rocks glass, ice
¾ oz. Irish Whiskey
¾ oz. Irish Mist
½ oz. Peppermint Schnapps

IRISH TEA...........................*Build*
Coffee mug, heated
1 oz. Irish Mist
½ oz. Irish Whiskey
Fill with hot tea
Lemon wedge garnish

ISLAND FLOWER......*Shake & Strain*
Cocktail glass, chilled
1½ oz. C. J. Wray Rum
½ oz. Blue Curaçao
½ oz. simple syrup
½ oz. fresh lime juice
¼ oz. grenadine

ITALIAN COFFEE.................*Build*
Coffee mug, heated
¾ oz. Sambuca
¾ oz. Amaretto di Saronno
Fill with hot coffee
Whipped cream garnish

ITALIAN MARGARITA
See MARGARITA, ITALIAN

ITALIAN ROOT BEER
See JERSEY ROOT BEER

ITALIAN SCREW
See GOLDEN SCREW

ITALIAN STINGER..............*Build*
Rocks glass, ice
1¼ oz. Brandy
¾ oz. Galliano

ITALIAN STALLION...............*Build*
Rocks glass, ice
1½ oz. Scotch
½ oz. Galliano

ITALIAN SUNRISE.................*Build*
Bucket glass, ice
1 oz. Amaretto di Saronno
Fill with orange juice
Float ½ oz. Creme de Cassis

ITALIAN VALIUM.................*Build*
Rocks glass, ice
1½ oz. Gin
½ oz. Amaretto di Saronno

JACKALOPE............*Shake & Strain*
House specialty glass, ice
¾ oz. Kahlua
¾ oz. Amaretto di Saronno
¾ oz. Myers's Jamaican Rum
3 oz. pineapple juice
Shake and strain
Float ½ oz. Brown Creme de Cacao

JACKARITA...............*Shake & Strain*
Cocktail glass, chilled
1¼ oz. Jack Daniels
¾ oz. Triple Sec
1¾ oz. sweet 'n' sour
Lime wedge garnish

JACK BENNY.......................*Build*
Rocks glass, ice
1½ oz. Jack Daniel's
½ oz. Bailey's Irish Cream
½ oz. Kahlua

JACK COLLINS.........*Shake & Strain*
a.k.a. APPLE COLLINS
Collins glass, ice
1 oz. Applejack
2 oz. sweet 'n' sour
Shake and strain
Fill with club soda
Orange slice and cherry garnish

JACK ROSE COCKTAIL
.........*Shake & Strain*
Cocktail glass, chilled
1 oz. Applejack
1½ oz. sweet 'n' sour
½ oz. grenadine

JADE..........................*Stir & Strain*
Cocktail glass, chilled
1½ oz. Light Rum
½ oz. Triple Sec
½ oz. Green Creme de Menthe
½ oz. Rose's lime juice

JÄGERITA...............*Shake & Strain*
Presentation shot glass, chilled
½ oz. Jägermeister
½ oz. Cuervo Especial Tequila
½ oz. Cointreau
¾ oz. fresh lime juice
Lime wedge garnish

JÄGER MONSTER..................*Build*
Bucket glass, ice
1¼ oz. Jägermeister
½ oz. Amaretto di Saronno
Fill with orange juice
Float ½ oz. grenadine

JÄGER SALSA............*Shake & Strain*
House specialty glass, ice
Salted rim optional
1¼ oz. Jägermeister
1-2 tsp. medium-hot salsa
Fill with Bloody Mary mix
Lime wedge and celery garnish

JAMAICA ME CRAZY (1).........*Build*
Bucket glass, ice
1½ oz. Myers's Jamaican Rum
½ oz. Tia Maria
Fill with pineapple juice

JAMAICA ME CRAZY (2)
.........*Blend with ice*
House specialty glass
1½ oz. Myers's Jamaican Rum
¾ oz. Blue Curaçao
2 oz. coconut cream
2 oz. pineapple juice
2 oz. orange juice

JAMAICAN BARBADOS BOMBER
............*Stir & Strain*
Presentation shot glass, chilled
1 oz. Myers's Jamaican Rum
1 oz. Mount Gay Barbados Rum
½ oz. Triple Sec
Dash Rose's lime juice
Lime wedge garnish

JAMAICAN COFFEE...............*Build*
Coffee mug, heated
¾ oz. Tia Maria
¾ oz. Myers's Jamaican Rum
Fill with hot coffee
Whipped cream garnish

JAMAICAN CRAWLER
.........*Shake & Strain*
Bucket glass, ice
1 oz. Light Rum
1 oz. Midori
3 oz. pineapple juice
½ oz. grenadine

JAMAICAN DUST..................*Build*
Presentation shot glass, chilled
⅓ fill Myers's Jamaican Rum
⅓ fill Tia Maria
⅓ fill pineapple juice

JAMAICAN HOLIDAY...........*Build*
Presentation shot glass, chilled
⅓ fill Myers's Jamaican Rum
⅓ fill Tia Maria
⅓ fill Banana Schnapps

JAMAICAN MARGARITA
See MARGARITA, JAMAICAN

JAMAICAN RUM COW
............*Blend with ice*
House specialty glass
1½ oz. Myers's Jamaican Rum
¾ cup milk
½ oz. simple syrup
2 dashes Angostura bitters

JAMAICAN SHAKE......*Blend with ice*
House specialty glass
¾ oz. Myers's Jamaican Rum
½ oz. Tia Maria
½ oz. Amaretto di Saronno
1-2 scoops vanilla ice cream
1 tsp. vanilla extract

JAMAICAN SPICE.................*Build*
Bucket glass, ice
1 oz. Captain Morgan's Spiced Rum
½ oz. Cinnamon Schnapps
Fill with ginger ale
Float ½ oz. Creme de Banana

JAMBA JUICE............*Shake & Strain*
Bucket glass, ice
¾ oz. Captain Morgan's Spiced Rum
¾ oz. Mount Gay Eclipse Rum
1 oz. cranberry juice
1 oz. orange juice
1 oz. pineapple juice
Shake and strain
Float ¾ oz. Myers's Jamaican Rum
Orange slice and cherry garnish

JAPANESE COCKTAIL
............*Stir & Strain*
Cocktail glass, chilled
1½ oz. Brandy
½ oz. orgeat syrup
2 dashes Angostura bitters
Lemon twist garnish

JAR JUICE...........................*Build*
Mason jar, ice
1 oz. Chambord
1 oz. Vodka
½ fill orange juice
½ fill pineapple juice

JELLY BEAN........................*Layer*
Presentation shot glass
½ fill Anisette
½ fill Blackberry Brandy

JENNY WALLBANGER............*Build*
Bucket glass, ice
1 oz. Vodka
½ fill orange juice
½ fill half & half cream
Float ½ oz. Galliano

JERSEY ROOT BEER...............*Build*
a.k.a. ITALIAN ROOT BEER
Highball glass, ice
1 oz. Galliano
Fill with cola

JOE CANOE..........................*Build*
a.k.a. JONKANOV
Bucket glass, ice
1 oz. Light Rum
Fill with orange juice
Float ½ oz. Galliano

JOHN COLLINS.........*Shake & Strain*
a.k.a. COLONEL COLLINS
Collins glass, ice
1 oz. Bourbon
2 oz. sweet 'n' sour
Shake and strain
Fill with club soda
Orange slice and cherry garnish

JOKE JUICE...............*Shake & Strain*
Cocktail glass, chilled
1¼ oz. Southern Comfort
½ oz. Triple Sec
½ oz. Rose's lime juice
½ oz. sweet 'n' sour

JULIA........................*Blend with ice*
House specialty Glass
1 oz. Light Rum
1 oz. Amaretto di Saronno
⅓ cup strawberries
1 oz. half & half cream
Strawberry garnish

JULIO'S BUTTERSCOTCH
.........*Blend with ice*
House specialty glass, chilled
½ oz. Kahlua
½ oz. Bailey's Irish Cream
½ oz. Butterscotch Schnapps
2 scoops vanilla ice cream

JUMBY BAY PUNCH......*Stir & Strain*
Cocktail glass, chilled
1½ oz. Jumby Bay Proprietor's Rum
1 oz. fresh lime juice
1 oz. simple syrup
3 dashes (9 drops) Angostura bitters
Sprinkle nutmeg
Orange wheel and cherry garnish

JUMP ME...............................*Build*
Bucket glass, ice
1½ oz. Myers's Jamaican Rum
2-3 dashes Angostura bitters
½ oz. fresh lime juice
4 oz. pineapple juice

JUNGLE JUICE........................*Build*
Bucket glass, ice
1 oz. Gin
1 oz. Vodka
½ fill orange juice
½ fill grapefruit juice

JUNGLE MILK........................*Build*
Coffee mug, heated
¾ oz. Bailey's Irish Cream
¾ oz. Creme de Banana
Fill with hot chocolate
Whipped cream garnish

KAHLUA CLUB.......................*Build*
Highball glass, ice
1 oz. Kahlua
Fill with club soda

KAHLUA & CREAM
See SOMBRERO

KAHLUA MINT.........*Shake or Blend*
Cocktail or house specialty glass, chilled
1 oz. Kahlua
½ oz. White Creme de Menthe
1½ oz. half & half cream

KAHLUA PIÑA COLADA
See PIÑA COLADA, KAHLUA

KAMIKAZE..................*Build or Stir*
Cocktail glass, chilled or rocks glass, ice
1½ oz. Vodka
½ oz. Triple Sec
½ oz. Rose's lime juice
Lime wedge garnish

KAMIKAZE, BLOODY
.................*Build or Stir*
Cocktail glass, chilled or rocks glass, ice
½ oz. Crystal Comfort
½ oz. Vodka
½ oz. Rose's lime juice
Stir and strain
Splash Cinnamon Schnapps
Lime wedge garnish

KAMIKAZE, BLUE.........*Build or Stir*
a.k.a. DEVINE WIND
Cocktail glass, chilled or rocks glass, ice
1½ oz. Vodka
½ oz. Blue Curaçao
½ oz. Rose's lime juice
Lime wedge garnish

KAMIKAZE, CITRON
............*Build or Stir*
Cocktail glass, chilled or rocks glass, ice
1½ oz. Absolut Citron
½ oz. Triple Sec
½ oz. Rose's lime juice
Lime wedge garnish

KAMIKAZE, CRANBERRY
............*Build or Stir*
Cocktail glass, chilled or rocks glass, ice
1½ oz. Vodka
½ oz. Triple Sec
½ oz. Rose's lime juice
½ oz. cranberry juice
Lime wedge garnish

KAMIKAZE, CRYSTAL
............*Build or Stir*
a. k. a. CRYSTAL KAMI
Cocktail glass, chilled or rocks glass, ice
1½ oz. Crystal Comfort
½ oz. Triple Sec
½ oz. Rose's lime juice
Lime wedge garnish

KAMIKAZE, FRENCH
...............*Build or Stir*
Cocktail glass, chilled or rocks glass, ice
1½ oz. Vodka
½ oz. Grand Marnier
¾ oz. fresh lime juice
Lime wedge garnish

KAMIKAZE, FUZZY......*Build or Stir*
Cocktail glass, chilled or rocks glass, ice
1½ oz. Vodka
½ oz. Peach Schnapps
¾ oz. Rose's lime juice
Lime wedge garnish

KAMIKAZE, KOKONUT
............*Build or Stir*
Cocktail glass, chilled or rocks glass, ice
2 oz. Malibu Rum
1 oz. pineapple juice
½ oz. sweet 'n' sour
Lime wedge garnish

KAMIKAZE, MELON
............*Build or Stir*
a.k.a. MELON-KAZI
Cocktail glass, chilled or rocks glass, ice
1 oz. Vodka
1 oz. Midori
½ oz. Rose's lime juice
Lime wedge garnish

KAMIKAZE, PURPLE
...........*Build or Stir*
a.k.a. PURPLE KAMI
Cocktail glass, chilled or rocks glass, ice
1½ oz. Vodka
½ oz. Chambord
Dash Rose's lime juice
Lime wedge garnish

KANGAROO
See VODKA MARTINI

KAPALUA BUTTERFLY
.........*Blend with ice*
House specialty glass, chilled
1¾ oz. Myers's Jamaican Rum
½ oz. grenadine
1½ oz. sweet 'n' sour
1½ oz. pineapple juice
1½ oz. coconut syrup
2 oz. orange juice

KATINKA...................*Stir & Strain*
Cocktail glass, chilled
1½ oz. Vodka
½ oz. Apricot Brandy
½ oz. Rose's lime juice
Mint sprig garnish optional

KENTUCKY MARGARITA
See MARGARITA, KENTUCKY

KENTUCKY SWAMPWATER
.....................*Build*
Bucket glass, ice
1½ oz. Bourbon
½ oz. Blue Curaçao
½ oz. fresh lime juice
Fill with orange juice
Lime wedge garnish

KEOKI COFFEE.....................*Build*
Coffee mug, heated
½ oz. Brandy
½ oz. Kahlua
½ oz. Creme de Cacao
Fill with hot coffee
Whipped cream garnish

KEOKI SHOOTER..................*Build*
Presentation shot glass, chilled
¼ fill Kahlua
¼ fill Brown Creme de Cacao
¼ fill Brandy
¼ fill hot coffee
Whipped cream garnish

KEY LIME COOLER
.........*Shake & Strain*
Cocktail glass, chilled
1 oz. Licor 43
½ oz. fresh lime juice
1 oz. half & half cream
Lime wheel garnish

KEY LIME MARGARITA
See MARGARITA, KEY LIME

KEY WEST...............*Shake & Strain*
House specialty glass, ice
½ oz. Bacardi Black Label Rum
½ oz. Myers's Jamaican Rum
½ oz. Creme de Banana
½ oz. Chambord
2 oz. sweet 'n' sour
2 oz. orange juice
Shake and strain
Fill with club soda
Orange slice and cherry garnish

KIDDY COCKTAIL......*Shake & Strain*
Cocktail glass, chilled
1 oz. grenadine
2 oz. sweet 'n' sour
Cherry garnish

KILLER KOOLAID......*Shake & Strain*
Cocktail glass, chilled
1 oz. Southern Comfort
1 oz. Midori
¾ oz. Creme de Noyaux
½ oz. cranberry juice

KILLER WHALE.........*Shake & Strain*
House specialty glass, ice
¾ oz. Vodka
¾ oz. Light Rum
½ oz. Chambord
½ oz. Triple Sec
½ fill cranberry juice
½ fill orange juice
Shake & strain
Fill with Seven-up

KING ALFONSE....................*Layer*
a.k.a. KING ALPHONSO
Cordial or pousse café glass
¾ fill Brown Creme de Cacao
¼ fill half & half cream

KING'S CUP............*Shake or Blend*
Cocktail or house specialty glass, chilled
1 oz. Galliano
½ oz. Amaretto di Saronno
1½ oz. half & half cream

KIR.............................*Build*
Wine glass or goblet
Fill with white wine
Float ½ oz. Creme de Cassis
Lemon twist garnish

KIR ROYALE......................*Build*
Champagne glass, chilled
Fill with Champagne
Float ½ oz. Creme de Cassis
Lemon twist garnish

KISS OF THE ISLANDS
.........*Shake or Blend*
House specialty glass, ice
1 oz. Myers's Jamaican Rum
1 oz. Creme de Banana
½ oz. Blue Curaçao
½ oz. coconut syrup
2 oz. pineapple juice
2 oz. orange juice
Shake and strain
Float ½ oz. Myers's Jamaican Rum
Orange slice and cherry garnish

KIWI..................................*Build*
Highball glass, ice
¾ oz. Strawberry Schnapps
¾ oz. Banana Schnapps
Fill with orange juice

KLONDIKE..................*Stir & Strain*
a.k.a. STAR COCKTAIL
Cocktail glass, chilled
1½ oz. Applejack
½ oz. Dry Vermouth
3 dashes Angostura bitters
1-2 dashes simple syrup optional
Lemon twist garnish

KNICKERBOCKER......*Shake & Strain*
Bucket glass, ice
1½ oz. Light Rum
½ oz. Triple Sec optional
½ oz. pineapple juice
½ oz. grenadine
1 oz. sweet 'n' sour
1 oz. orange juice

KNICKERBOCKER KNOCKER
.........*Shake & Strain*
House specialty glass, ice
¾ oz. Midori
¾ oz. Peach Schnapps
¾ oz. sweet 'n' sour
1½ oz. orange juice
1½ oz. cranberry juice
Shake and strain
Float ½ oz. Creme de Banana
Orange slice and cherry garnish

KNOCKOUT...............*Stir & Strain*
Cocktail glass, chilled
¾ oz. Gin
¾ oz. Pernod
¾ oz. Dry Vermouth
3 dashes White Creme de Menthe
Lemon twist garnish

KOALA FLOAT.........*Blend with ice*
House specialty glass
1 oz. Kahlua
1 oz. Bailey's Irish Cream
2 oz. coconut syrup
3 oz. pineapple juice
Pineapple wedge garnish

KOKONUT KAMIKAZE
See KAMIKAZE, KOKONUT

KOOL AID (1)..............*Build or Shake*
Cocktail glass, chilled or highball glass, ice
½ oz. Vodka
½ oz. Midori
½ oz. Amaretto di Saronno
1½ oz. cranberry juice

KOOL AID (2)...........*Build or Shake*
Cocktail glass, chilled or highball glass, ice
½ oz. Midori
½ oz. Amaretto di Saronno
½ oz. Southern Comfort
¼ oz. Vodka
¼ oz. grenadine
1 oz. cranberry juice

KUWAITI COOLER
.........*Shake & Strain*
Bucket glass, ice
1 oz. Midori
1 oz. Key Largo Schnapps
2 oz. sweet 'n' sour
Shake and strain
Fill with club soda

LA BAMBA...............*Shake & Strain*
Coupette glass, chilled
1¼ oz. Sauza Conmemorativo Tequila
¾ oz. Cointreau
1½ oz. pineapple juice
1½ oz. orange juice
Shake and strain
Float ¼ oz. grenadine

LADY MADONNA...............*Build*
Brandy snifter, ice
1½ oz. Dubonnet Rouge
1½ oz. Dry Vermouth
Lemon twist

LAGER AND LIME...............*Build*
Beer glass, chilled
1½ oz. Rose's lime juice
Fill draft lager
Note: *Substitute black currant juice for*
Rose's to make a **LAGER AND**
BLACK

LAGNIAPPE...........................*Build*
Rocks glass
Half a fresh peach
Fill with crushed ice
1½ oz. Bourbon
Note: *The "lagniappe", or "bonus", is the*
bourbon-soaked peach.

LAKE STREET LEMONADE
.....................*Build*
Bucket glass, ice
1½ oz. Vodka
½ oz. Amaretto di Saronno
Fill with lemonade
Lemon wedge garnish

La MOSCA...........................*Build*
a.k.a. SAMBUCA CON MOSCA
Cordial or Sherry glass
Fill with Sambuca
Garnish with 3 coffee beans

LANDSLIDE...........................*Layer*
Presentation shot glass, chilled
⅓ fill Creme de Banana
⅓ fill Myers's Rum Cream
⅓ fill Grand Marnier

L.A.P.D......................*Shake & Strain*
Presentation shot glass, chilled
1 oz. Sauza Hornitos Tequila
½ oz. Blue Curaçao
¼ oz. grenadine

LARCHMONT..............*Stir & Strain*
Cocktail glass, chilled or rocks glass, ice
1½ oz. Light Rum
¾ oz. Grand Marnier
½ oz. Rose's lime juice
Orange peel garnish

LATIN MANHATTAN
See MANHATTAN, LATIN

LEAF.......................*Shake or Blend*
Cocktail or house specialty glass, chilled
1 oz. Midori
½ oz. Light Rum
1½ oz. half & half cream

LEANING TOWER
.........*Shake & Strain*
House specialty glass, ice
1 oz. Captain Morgan's Spiced Rum
1 oz. Creme de Banana
1 oz. coconut syrup
2 oz. orange juice
2 oz. pineapple juice
Shake and strain
Float ½ oz. grenadine
Orange slice and cherry garnish

Le BISTRO...........................*Build*
Cappuccino cup, heated
¾ oz. Benedictine D.O.M.
¾ oz. Brandy
Fill with hot espresso coffee
Steam mixture of 4 oz. milk and ½ oz. each
of Frangelico and Amaretto di Saronno.
Spoon on frothed mixture
Shaved chocolate garnish

LEFT BANK...........................*Build*
Rocks glass, ice
1 oz. Bailey's Irish Cream
1 oz. Chambord

LEISURE SUIT.........*Shake & Strain*
House specialty glass, ice
1 oz. Galliano
1 oz. Creme de Banana
2 oz. pineapple juice
2 oz. orange juice
2 oz. cranberry juice

LEMON DROP (1)......*Shake & Strain*
Cocktail glass, chilled
Sugar rim optional
1½ oz. Stolichnaya Vodka
½ oz. Triple Sec
½ oz. fresh lemon juice
Lemon twist garnish

LEMON DROP (2)......*Shake & Strain*
Bucket glass, ice
1¼ oz. Vodka
2 oz. sweet 'n' sour
Shake and strain
½ fill with club soda
½ fill with Seven-up

LEMON DROP (3)......*Shake & Strain*
Cocktail glass, chilled
1 oz. Vodka
¾ oz. Triple Sec
¼ oz. simple syrup
¼ oz. Rose's lime juice
½ oz. sweet 'n' sour
Shake and strain
Splash Seven-up

LEMONGRAD........................*Build*
Highball glass, ice
1¼ oz. Stolichnaya Limonnaya
Fill with cranberry juice

LEMON SPORTSMAN............*Build*
Bucket glass, ice
1 oz. Stolichnaya Vodka
Fill with lemonade
Float ½ oz. Stolichnaya Limonnaya

LEMON TOP..........................*Build*
Beer glass, chilled
Fill ⁹⁄₁₀ draught lager
Fill with Seven-up

LEMON TREE TANTALIZER
..........*Blend with ice*
House specialty glass, chilled
1½ oz. Stolichnaya Limonnaya
2 scoops lemon sorbet
Blend with crushed ice
Lemon wedge garnish

LENA COCKTAIL.........*Stir & Strain*
Cocktail glass, chilled
1½ oz. Bourbon
¼ oz. Sweet Vermouth
¼ oz. Dry Vermouth
¼ oz. Campari Aperitivo
¼ oz. Galliano
Lemon twist garnish

LEPRECHAUN.......................*Build*
Highball glass, ice
¾ oz. Peach Schnapps
¾ oz. Blue Curaçao
Fill with orange juice

LETHAL INJECTION
.........*Shake & Strain*
Rocks glass, chilled
½ oz. Captain Morgan's Spiced Rum
½ oz. Malibu Rum
½ oz. Creme de Noyaux
½ oz. Bacardi Black Label Rum
¾ oz. orange juice
¾ oz. pineapple juice

LIAM'S PASSION.........*Blend with ice*
House specialty glass, chilled
2 oz. Myers's Jamaican Rum
2 oz. coconut syrup
4½ oz. passion fruit juice

LIGHTHOUSE.......................*Build*
Rocks glass, ice
½ oz. Tequila
½ oz. Kahlua
½ oz. Peppermint Schnapps
½ oz. 151 Rum

LILLET CHAMPAGNE ROYALE
........................*Build*
Champagne glass, chilled
2 oz. Lillet Blonde
Fill with Champagne
½ oz. Creme de Cassis
Lemon twist

LOBOTOMY............*Shake & Strain*
Presentation shot glass, chilled
½ oz. Amaretto di Saronno
½ oz. Chambord
½ oz. pineapple juice
Shake and strain
Fill with Champagne

LOCH LOMOND............*Stir & Strain*
Cocktail glass, chilled
1½ oz. Scotch
2 dashes simple syrup
Dash Angostura bitters
Lemon twist garnish

LOCO EN LA CABEZA
.........*Shake & Strain*
Cocktail glass, chilled
1½ oz. Tequila
½ oz. Triple Sec
1½ oz. orange juice
½ oz. Rose's lime juice
½ oz. grenadine
Lime wedge garnish

LONG BEACH ICED TEA
See ICED TEA, LONG BEACH

LONG ISLAND ICED TEA
See ICED TEA, LONG ISLAND

LOUISIANA SHOOTER.........*Build*
Presentation shot glass, chilled
1 small raw oyster
1½ oz. Stolichnaya Pertsovka
¼ tsp. prepared horseradish
2-3 dashes Tabasco sauce

LOUVRE ME ALONE...............*Build*
Cappuccino cup, heated
½ oz. Grand Marnier
½ oz. V.S. Cognac
½ oz. Tia Maria
¾ fill hot espresso coffee
Spoon on frothed milk
Shaved chocolate garnish

LUAU...................................*Build*
Bucket glass, ice
1 oz. Malibu Rum
1 oz. Maui Schnapps
Fill with pineapple juice
Orange slice and cherry garnish

LYNCHBURG LEMONADE
.........*Shake & Strain*

Bucket glass, ice
1 oz. Jack Daniel's
¾ oz. Triple Sec
1½ oz. sweet 'n' sour
Shake and strain
Fill with Seven-Up

MACINTOSH PRESS
....................*Build*

Highball glass, ice
1 oz. Apple Schnapps
½ fill ginger ale
½ fill club soda

MACKENZIE GOLD...............*Build*
Highball glass, ice
1½ oz. Yukon Jack
Fill with grapefruit juice

MADONNA'S BRASSIERRE
....................*Build*

Presentation shot glass, chilled
¼ fill Stolichnaya Pertsovka
¼ fill Cherry Schnapps
¼ fill Peppermint Schnapps
¼ fill Bailey's Irish Cream

MADRAS.............................*Build*
Highball glass, ice
1 oz. Vodka
½ fill orange juice
½ fill cranberry juice

MAD RUSSIAN MARGARITA
See MARGARITA, MAD RUSSIAN

MADTOWN MILKSHAKE
.........*Blend with ice*

House specialty glass, ice
1 oz. Bailey's Irish cream
1 oz. Chambord
¾ oz. Frangelico
2 oz. half & half cream
Whipped cream garnish

MAIDEN'S PRAYER
.........*Shake & Strain*

Cocktail glass, chilled
1½ oz. Gin
½ oz. Triple Sec
1 oz. sweet 'n' sour
Dash orange juice
Dash Angostura bitters

MAI TAI.................*Shake & Strain*
House specialty glass, ice
1½ oz. Light Rum
½ oz. Orgeat syrup or Creme de Noyaux
½ oz. Triple Sec
2 oz. sweet 'n' sour
Fresh fruit garnish

MALIBU BEACH....................*Build*
Bucket glass, ice
1½ oz. Malibu Rum
¾ oz. Myers's Jamaican Rum
Fill with papaya juice

MALIBU FIZZ........................*Build*
Bucket glass, ice
1 oz. Malibu Rum
¾ oz. Midori
Fill with ginger ale
Float ½ oz. Bailey's Irish Cream

MALIBU RUNNER.................*Build*
Tall specialty glass, ice
1 oz. Malibu Rum
¾ oz. Amaretto di Saronno
Fill with pineapple juice
Float ½ oz. grenadine

MALIBU SUNSET.................*Build*
Bucket glass, ice
1½ oz. Malibu Rum
½ oz. Peach Schnapps
Fill with orange juice
Float ½ oz. grenadine

MAMA CITRON....................*Build*
Rocks glass, ice
1½ oz. Absolut Citron
½ oz. Amaretto di Saronno

MAMIE TAYLOR.................*Build*
Highball glass, ice
1 oz. Scotch
Fill with ginger ale
Lemon wedge garnish
Note: *The following drink names are made with the products listed using the above recipe:*
MAMIE'S SISTER – Gin
MAMIE'S SOUTHERN SISTER – Bourbon
SUSIE TAYLOR – Light Rum

MANDARIN TWIST COFFEE
....................*Build*

Coffee mug, heated
1 oz. Grand Marnier
1 oz. Brown Creme de Cacao
¼ oz. Cointreau
Fill with hot coffee
Whipped cream garnish

MANGO BANGO.................*Build*
Highball glass, ice
1 oz. Mohala Mango Liqueur
½ fill cranberry juice
½ fill grapefruit juice

MANGO MARGARITA
See MARGARITA, MANGO

MANGO MONSOON...........*Build*
Highball glass, ice
1 oz. Mohala Mango Liqueur
½ oz. Vodka
Fill with pineapple juice

MANHATTAN...........*Build or Stir*
Cocktail glass, chilled or rocks glass, ice
Dash Angostura bitters optional
½ oz. Sweet Vermouth
1½ oz. Bourbon
Cherry garnish
  Note: *Manhattans originally were made*
        with rye whiskey.
The following drink names are made with
the products listed using the above recipe:
ROB ROY – Scotch
PADDY – Irish Whiskey

MANHATTAN, BRANDY
............*Build or Stir*
a.k.a. DELMONICO
Cocktail glass, chilled or rocks glass, ice
½ oz. Sweet Vermouth
1½ oz. Brandy
Dash Angostura bitters optional
Cherry garnish

MANHATTAN, DRY......*Build or Stir*
Cocktail glass, chilled or rocks glass, ice
Dash Angostura bitters optional
¼ oz. Dry Vermouth
1½ oz. Bourbon
Green olives or lemon twist garnish

MANHATTAN, DRY BRANDY
............*Build or Stir*
Cocktail glass, chilled or rocks glass, ice
Dash Angostura bitters optional
¼ oz. Dry Vermouth
1½ oz. Brandy
Green olives or lemon twist garnish

MANHATTAN, LATIN
............*Stir & Strain*
Cocktail glass, chilled or rocks glass, ice
2 dashes Angostura bitters optional
¼ oz. Sweet Vermouth
¼ oz. Dry Vermouth
1½ oz. Light Rum
Lemon twist garnish

MANHATTAN, NEW ORLEAN'S
............*Build or Stir*
Cocktail glass, chilled or rocks glass, ice
Swirl ½ oz. Frangelico; discard excess
½ oz. Sweet Vermouth
1½ oz. Bourbon or Rye Whiskey
Cherry garnish

MANHATTAN, PERFECT
............*Build or Stir*
Cocktail glass, chilled or rocks glass, ice
Dash Angostura bitters optional
¼ oz. Dry Vermouth
¼ oz. Sweet Vermouth
1½ oz. Bourbon
Lemon twist garnish

MANHATTAN, PERFECT BRANDY
............*Build or Stir*
Cocktail glass, chilled or rocks glass, ice
Dash Angostura bitters optional
¼ oz. Dry Vermouth
¼ oz. Sweet Vermouth
1½ oz. Brandy
Lemon twist garnish

MANHATTAN, PERFECT SOUTHERN
  COMFORT...................*Build or Stir*
Cocktail glass, chilled or rocks glass, ice
¼ oz. Dry Vermouth
¼ oz. Sweet Vermouth
1½ oz. Southern Comfort
Lemon twist garnish

MANHATTAN, SOUTHERN
  COMFORT...................*Build or Stir*
Cocktail glass, chilled or rocks glass, ice
¼ oz. Dry Vermouth
1½ oz. Southern Comfort
Cherry garnish

MARGARITA...........*Shake or Blend*
Cocktail or house specialty glass, chilled
Salted rim optional
1 oz. Tequila
½ oz. Triple Sec
1½ oz. sweet 'n' sour
Dash orange juice optional
Rose's lime juice optional
Lime wedge garnish

MARGARITA AMORE
........*Shake or Blend*
Cocktail or house specialty glass, chilled
Salted rim optional
1¼ oz. El Tesoro Plata Tequila
¾ oz. Amaretto di Saronno
½ oz. Blue Curaçao
1 oz. sweet 'n' sour
1 oz. fresh lime juice
Lime wedge garnish

MARGARITA, APPLE
.........Shake or Blend
Cocktail or house specialty glass, chilled
Cinnamon-sugar rim optional
1 oz. Tequila
1 oz. Apple Schnapps
1½ oz. sweet 'n' sour
½ oz. apple juice or cider
1 tbsp. apple sauce optional
Apple slice garnish

MARGARITA, BLACK GOLD
.........Shake or Blend
Cocktail or house specialty glass, chilled
Salted rim optional
1¼ oz. Sauza Conmemorativo Tequila
1 oz. Lime flavored Vodka
¾ oz. Chambord
1¼ oz. fresh lime juice
Splash Rose's lime juice optional
Lime wedge garnish

MARGARITA, BLUE
.........Shake or Blend
Cocktail or house specialty glass, chilled
Salted rim optional
1 oz. Tequila
½ oz. Blue Curaçao
1½ oz. sweet 'n' sour
Lime wedge garnish
   Note: *Use Cuervo Gold to make a*
   MIDNIGHT MARGARITA

MARGARITA, BLUE MOON
.........Blend with ice
House specialty glass, chilled
Salted rim optional
1½ oz. Sauza Conmemorativo Tequila
¾ oz. Blue Curaçao
½ oz. Rose's lime juice
1½ oz. sweet 'n' sour
1-2 scoops lemon sorbet
Lime wheel garnish

MARGARITA, CACTUS ROSE
.........Blend with ice
House specialty glass, chilled
Sugar rim optional
1 oz. Cuervo Especial Tequila
½ oz. Grand Marnier
½ oz. Chambord
¼ cup frozen raspberries
2 tbsp. prickly pear marmalade
2½ oz. sweet 'n' sour
1 oz. cranberry juice
½ oz. Rose's lime juice
Prickly pear garnish

MARGARITA, CADILLAC
.........Shake & Strain
Cocktail or house specialty glass, chilled
Salted rim optional
1½ oz. Cuervo 1800 Tequila
¾ oz. Grand Marnier
1½ oz. sweet 'n' sour
½ oz. cranberry juice optional
Lime wedge garnish

MARGARITA, CAJUN (1)
.........Shake & Strain
Cocktail or house specialty glass, chilled
Salted rim optional
1¾ oz. jalapeño-steeped Tequila
1-2 dashes Tabasco sauce
2 pinches ground black pepper
2 oz. sweet 'n' sour
Small jalapeño peppers garnish

MARGARITA, CAJUN (2)
.........Shake & Strain
Cocktail or house specialty glass, chilled
Salted rim optional
1 oz. Stolichnaya Pertsovka
¾ oz. Cuervo Especial Tequila
½ oz. Triple Sec optional
1-2 dashes Tabasco sauce
2 pinches ground black pepper
4-6 drops jalapeño pepper juice
2 oz. sweet 'n' sour
Small jalapeño peppers garnish

MARGARITA, CATALINA
.........Shake or Blend
Cocktail or house specialty glass, chilled
Salted rim optional
1¼ oz. Tequila
½ oz. Blue Curaçao
½ oz. Peach Schnapps
2 oz. sweet 'n' sour
Lime wedge garnish

MARGARITA, CHINACOUT
.........Shake & Strain
Cocktail or house specialty glass, chilled
Salted rim optional
1¼ oz. Chinaco Añejo Tequila
¾ oz. Royale Montaine
1½ oz. sweet 'n' sour
Lime wedge garnish

MARGARITA, FRUIT
.........*Blend with ice*
House specialty glass, chilled
Sugar rim optional
1 oz. Tequila
½ oz. Triple Sec
1½ oz. sweet 'n' sour
½ cup of requested fruit
Dash orange juice optional
Rose's lime juice optional
  Note: *Among the popular fruit choices are:*
    apple, **apricot**, **banana**, **kiwi**,
    melon, **peach**, **raspberry**,
    strawberry and **watermelon**.

MARGARITA, GEORGIA
.........*Shake or Blend*
Cocktail or house specialty glass, chilled
1 oz. Tequila
¾ oz. Peach Schnapps
1½ oz. sweet 'n' sour
Lime wedge garnish

MARGARITA, GOLD
.........*Shake or Blend*
Cocktail or house specialty glass, chilled
Salted rim optional
1 oz. Cuervo Especial Tequila
½ oz. Grand Marnier
1½ oz. sweet 'n' sour
Lime wedge garnish

MARGARITA, ITALIAN
.........*Shake or Blend*
Cocktail or house specialty glass, chilled
Sugar rim optional
1¼ oz. oz. Amaretto di Saronno
½ oz. Gold Tequila
½ oz. Triple Sec
2 oz. sweet 'n' sour
Orange slice, cherry and lime garnish

MARGARITA, JAMAICAN
.........*Shake or Blend*
Cocktail or house specialty glass, chilled
1¼ oz. Myers's Jamaican Rum
½ oz. Triple Sec
1½ oz. sweet 'n' sour
Lime wedge garnish

MARGARITA, KENTUCKY
.........*Shake or Blend*
Cocktail or house specialty glass, chilled
1½ oz. Bourbon
½ oz. Triple Sec
1½ oz. sweet 'n' sour
Lime wedge garnish

MARGARITA, KEY LIME
.........*Shake or Blend*
Cocktail or house specialty glass, chilled
Salted rim optional
1 oz. Tequila
1 oz. Lime-flavored vodka
½ oz. Triple Sec
¼ oz. Rose's lime juice
¼ oz. sweet 'n' sour
Lime wedge garnish

MARGARITA, MAD RUSSIAN
.........*Shake or Blend*
Cocktail or house specialty glass, chilled
Salted rim optional
1 oz. Cuervo Especial Tequila
¾ oz. Red Curaçao
½ oz. Grand Marnier
2 oz. sweet 'n' sour
Lime wedge garnish

MARGARITA, MAXIMILIAN
.........*Shake & Strain*
Cocktail glass, chilled
Salted rim optional
1¼ oz. El Tesoro Muy Añejo Tequila
¾ oz. Grand Marnier Centcinquintenaire
1½ oz. fresh lime juice
Lime wedge garnish

MARGARITA, MANGO
.........*Shake or Blend*
a.k.a. MANGORITA
Cocktail or house specialty glass, chilled
Salted rim optional
1¼ oz. Tequila
1 oz. Mohala Mango Liqueur
1½ oz. sweet 'n' sour
½ oz. Rose's lime juice
Lime wedge garnish

MARGARITA, MAUI
.........*Shake or Blend*
House specialty glass, chilled
Salted rim optional
1¼ oz. Tequila
¾ oz. Maui Schnapps
1½ oz. sweet 'n' sour
1½ oz. cranberry juice
Lime wedge garnish

MARGARITA, MELON
.........*Shake or Blend*
a.k.a. GREEN IGUANA
Cocktail or house specialty glass, chilled
Salted rim optional
1 oz. Midori
1 oz. Tequila
1½ oz. sweet 'n' sour
Lime wedge garnish

MARGARITA, MIDNIGHT
See MARGARITA, BLUE

MARGARITA, MIDNIGHT MADNESS
............*Blend with ice*
House specialty glass, chilled
Salted rim optional
Two blender canisters required
  Step one/canister one
¾ oz. Cuervo Especial Tequila
¾ oz. Blue Curaçao
1½ oz. sweet 'n' sour
Blend with ice
Pour into glass
  Step two/canister two
¾ oz. Cuervo Especial Tequila
¾ oz. Red Curaçao
1½ oz. sweet 'n' sour
Blend with ice
Pour on top of first drink
Lime wedge garnish

MARGARITA, MOUNT FUGI
.........*Shake or Blend*
Cocktail or house specialty glass, chilled
2 oz. Sake
½ oz. Triple Sec
2 oz. sweet 'n' sour
Lemon wheel garnish

MARGARITA, ORANGE
.........*Shake or Blend*
Cocktail or house specialty glass, chilled
Sugar rim optional
1 oz. Tequila
½ oz. Triple Sec
1½ oz. orange juice
Lime wedge garnish

MARGARITA, PEAR
............*Blend with ice*
a.k.a. PEARITA
House specialty glass, chilled
Salted rim optional
1½ oz. Tequila
½ oz. Triple Sec
1 canned whole Bartlett pear
2 oz. lime juice
½ oz. lemon juice
Lime wheel garnish

MARGARITA, PINEAPPLE
.........*Blend with ice*
a.k.a. PIÑARITA
Cocktail or house specialty glass, chilled
1¼ oz. Tequila
¾ oz. Cointreau
1½ oz. pineapple juice
¼ cup pineapple chunks optional
Lime wedge garnish

MARGARITA, PURPLE
.........*Shake or Blend*
a.k.a. PURPLE GECKO
Cocktail or house specialty glass, chilled
Salted rim optional
1½ oz. Tequila
½ oz. Blue Curaçao
½ oz. Red Curaçao
½ oz. Rose's lime juice
1 oz. cranberry juice
1 oz. sweet 'n' sour
Lime wedge garnish

MARGARITA, RASPBERRY
............*Blend with ice*
House specialty glass, chilled
Sugar rim optional
1 oz. Cuervo Especial Tequila
½ oz. Grand Marnier
½ oz. Chambord
½ cup raspberries
1 oz. sweet 'n' sour
Lime wedge garnish

MARGARITA, RED HOT
.........*Shake or Blend*
Cocktail or house specialty glass, chilled
Salted rim optional
1½ oz. Cuervo Especial Tequila
¾ oz. Cinnamon Schnapps
1½ oz. sweet 'n' sour
Lime wedge garnish

MARGARITA, ROLLS ROYCE
.........*Shake & Strain*
Cocktail or house specialty glass, chilled
Salted rim optional
1½ oz. Chinaco Añejo Tequila
¾ oz. Grand Marnier
1½ oz. sweet 'n' sour
Splash orange juice
Lime wedge garnish

MARGARITA, ROSARITA
.........*Shake & Strain*
House specialty glass, chilled
Salted rim optional
1¼ oz. Sauza Conmemorativo Tequila
¾ oz. Grand Marnier
1½ oz. sweet 'n' sour
½ oz. cranberry juice
½ oz. Rose's lime juice
Lime wedge garnish

MARGARITA, SONORAN
.........*Shake & Strain*
Cocktail or house specialty glass, chilled
Salted rim optional
1 oz. Cuervo 1800 Tequila
¾ oz. Grand Marnier
1½ oz. sweet 'n' sour
Lime wedge garnish

MARGARITA, TUACA
.........Shake or Blend
Cocktail or house specialty glass, chilled
1 oz. Tuaca
1 oz. Tequila
½ oz. Triple Sec optional
1½ oz. sweet 'n' sour
Lime wedge garnish

MARGARITA, VINTNER'S
.........Shake or Blend
House specialty glass, chilled
Salted rim optional
3 oz. dry white wine
½ oz. Triple Sec
2 oz. sweet 'n' sour
½ oz. Rose's lime juice
½ oz. orange juice
Lime and orange wheel garnish

MARGARITA, VIRGIN
.........Shake & Strain
Cocktail or house specialty glass, ice
Salted rim optional
2 oz. sweet 'n' sour
1 oz. orange juice
½ oz. Rose's lime juice
Lime wedge garnish
   Note: *If available, substitute 1 oz. orange juice*
      with ¾ oz. non-alcoholic Triple Sec.

MARITIME SUNRISE............*Build*
Brandy snifter, ice
2 oz. Vodka
4 oz. grapefruit juice
1 oz. cranberry juice
Float ½ oz. Cherry Schnapps

MARQUIS...........................*Build*
Rocks glass, ice
¾ oz. B. & B. Liqueur
¾ oz. Kahlua
¼ oz. Triple Sec
½ oz. half & half cream

MARTINI.....................*Build or Stir*
Cocktail glass, chilled or rocks glass, ice
5-8 drops Dry Vermouth
1½ oz. Gin
Olives or lemon twist garnish

MARTINI, BLACK.........*Build or Stir*
Cocktail glass, chilled or rocks glass, ice
1½ oz. Stolichnaya Cristall Vodka
½ oz. Chambord
Lemon twist garnish

MARTINI, BOSTON......*Build or Stir*
Cocktail glass, chilled or rocks glass, ice
2-3 dashes Dry Vermouth
2 oz. Gin
Anchovy-wrapped or almond-stuffed olives garnish

MARTINI, BUCKEYE......*Build or Stir*
Cocktail glass, chilled or rocks glass, ice
2-3 dashes Dry Vermouth
2 oz. Gin
Black olives garnish

MARTINI, CAJUN (1)......*Build or Stir*
Cocktail glass, chilled or rocks glass, ice
2-3 dashes Dry Vermouth
2-3 dashes Sweet Vermouth
¾ oz. Gin
¾ oz. jalapeño-steeped gin
Small jalapeño peppers garnish

MARTINI, CAJUN (2)......*Build or Stir*
Cocktail glass, chilled or rocks glass, ice
2-3 dashes Dry Vermouth
2 oz. Gin
Cooked crawfish garnish
   Note: *Steep crawfish in Absolut Peppar prior*
      to cooking.

MARTINI, CAJUN KING
............Build or Stir
Cocktail glass, chilled or rocks glass, ice
1-2 dashes Dry Vermouth
½ oz. Absolut Citron
1½ oz. Absolut Peppar
Small jalapeño peppers garnish

MARTINI, DRY............*Build or Stir*
Cocktail glass, chilled or rocks glass, ice
3-4 drops Dry Vermouth
1½ oz. Gin
Olives or lemon twist garnish

MARTINI, DRY VODKA
............Build or Stir
Cocktail glass, chilled or rocks glass, ice
3-4 drops Dry Vermouth
1½ oz. Vodka
Olives or lemon twist garnish

MARTINI, DUTCH.........*Build or Stir*
Cocktail glass, chilled or rocks glass, ice
¼ oz. Dry Vermouth
1½ oz. Genever Gin
Lemon twist garnish

MARTINI, EXTRA DRY
............Build or Stir
Cocktail glass, chilled or rocks glass, ice
1 drop or no Dry Vermouth
1½ oz. Gin
Olives or lemon twist garnish

MARTINI, EXTRA DRY VODKA
............*Build or Stir*
Cocktail glass, chilled or rocks glass, ice
1 drop or no Dry Vermouth
1½ oz. Vodka
Olives or lemon twist garnish

MARTINI, FIDEL'S.........*Build or Stir*
Cocktail glass, chilled or rocks glass, ice
1½ oz. Stolichnaya Vodka
2-3 drops Banana Schnapps
Banana slice garnish

MARTINI, FRENCH......*Build or Stir*
a.k.a. PAISLEY, GOLDEN DROP
Cocktail glass, chilled or rocks glass, ice
¼ oz. Scotch
¼ oz. Dry Vermouth optional
1½ oz. Gin
Lemon twist garnish

MARTINI, HOT............*Build or Stir*
Cocktail glass, chilled or rocks glass, ice
¼ oz. Dry Vermouth
2-3 dashes pickled jalapeño juice
2-3 dashes fresh lime juice
2 oz. Stolichnaya Vodka
Jalapeño-stuffed olive garnish

MARTINI, NUTCRACKER
............*Build or Stir*
Cocktail glass, chilled or rocks glass, ice
1-2 dashes Frangelico
1½ oz. Vodka
Lemon twist garnish

MARTINI, PERFECT......*Build or Stir*
a.k.a. PERFECT COCKTAIL
Cocktail glass, chilled or rocks glass, ice
Dash Angostura bitters optional
1¾ oz. Gin
¼ oz. Sweet Vermouth
¼ oz. Dry Vermouth
Lemon twist garnish

MARTINI, RIVIERA......*Build or Stir*
Cocktail glass, chilled or rocks glass, ice
2 oz. Gin
½ oz. Sweet Vermouth
Dash orange flower water
Dash Pernod
Dash Angostura bitters

MARTINI, SAKE.........*Build or Stir*
a.k.a. SAKINI
Cocktail glass, chilled or rocks glass, ice
½ oz. Sake
1½ oz. Gin
Olive garnish

MARTINI, SPANISH......*Build or Stir*
Cocktail glass, chilled or rocks glass, ice
½ oz. Dry Sack Sherry
1½ oz. Gin
Lemon twist garnish

MARTINI, STRAWBERRY
............*Build or Stir*
Cocktail glass, chilled or rocks glass, ice
½ oz. Chambraise
1½ oz. Dry Gin
Fresh strawberry garnish

MARTINI, VODKA.........*Build or Stir*
Cocktail glass, chilled or rocks glass, ice
5-8 drops Dry Vermouth
1½ oz. Vodka
Olives or lemon twist garnish

MAUI BREEZER.........*Blend with ice*
House specialty glass, chilled
1½ oz. Amaretto di Saronno
½ oz. Triple Sec
½ oz. Brandy
1 oz. sweet 'n' sour
2 oz. orange juice
2 oz. guava juice
Fresh fruit garnish

MAXIMILIAN MARGARITA
See MARGARITA, MAXIMILIAN

MAXIM'S A LONDRES
.........*Shake & Strain*
Champagne glass, chilled
1½ oz. Brandy
½ oz. Cointreau
½ oz. orange juice
Shake and strain
Fill with Champagne
Orange twist garnish

MEADOWLARK LEMON
............*Stir & Strain*
Cocktail glass, chilled
1½ oz. Stolichnaya Cristall Vodka
½ oz. Cointreau
½ oz. fresh lemon juice
Lemon wedge garnish

MEDITERRANEAN FREEZE
.........*Blend with ice*
House specialty glass, chilled
1 oz. Vodka
¾ oz. Midori
½ oz. Peach Schnapps
2 oz. sweet 'n' sour
3 oz. orange juice
Orange slice and cherry garnish

MEISTER-BATION (1)
........*Shake & Strain*
Rocks glass, chilled
1 oz. Jägermeister
½ oz. Creme de Banana
1 oz. half & half cream
1 oz. Piña Colada mix
Packaged condom garnish

MEISTER-BATION (2)
...........*Blend with ice*
Rocks glass, chilled
1½ oz. Jägermeister
¾ oz. Creme de Banana
1 oz. half & half cream
1 oz. Piña Colada mix
Packaged condom garnish

MELLONAIRE........*Shake & Strain*
Cocktail glass, chilled
1 oz. Midori
½ oz. Creme de Banana
½ oz. Triple Sec
1½ oz. sweet 'n' sour

MELLOW DRAMATIC...........*Build*
Presentation shot glass, chilled
⅓ fill Chambord
⅓ fill White Creme de Cacao
⅓ fill Bailey's Irish Cream

MELON BALL (1).................*Build*
Highball glass, ice
1 oz. Midori
½ oz. Vodka
Fill with orange juice

MELON BALL (2)......*Shake & Strain*
Rocks glass, chilled
1½ oz. Midori
½ oz. Vodka
½ oz. orange juice
½ oz. pineapple juice

MELON BALL COOLER
........*Shake & Strain*
House specialty glass, ice
1½ oz. Midori
¾ oz. Vodka
1 oz. pineapple juice
1 oz. orange juice
Shake and strain
Fill with ginger ale

MELON BREEZE....................*Build*
Highball glass, ice
1 oz. Midori
½ oz. Vodka
½ fill cranberry juice
½ fill pineappple juice

MELON GRIND....................*Build*
Bucket glass, ice
¾ oz. Midori
½ oz. Vodka
½ oz. Light Rum
Fill with pineapple juice

MELON KAMIKAZE
See KAMIKAZE, MELON

MELON MARGARITA
See MARGARITA, MELON

MELON MOOSE.................*Build*
Bucket glass, ice
¾ oz. Vodka
¾ oz. Midori
Fill with pineapple juice
Float 1 oz. Myers's Jamaican Rum

MELON SCOOP........*Blend with ice*
House specialty glass, chilled
1 oz. Mount Gay Eclipse Rum
1 oz. Midori
1-2 scoops vanilla ice cream
Orange slice and cherry garnish

MEL'S CHOCOLATE
BUTTERSCOTCH MILKSHAKE
...........*Blend with ice*
House specialty glass
1½ oz. Kahlua optional
¾ oz. Myers's Jamaican Rum optional
2-3 scoops vanilla ice cream
4 oz. whole milk
2 oz. butterscotch topping
1 oz. chocolate syrup
Whipped cream garnish

MEL'S CHOC/PB/NANA SHAKE
...........*Blend with ice*
House specialty glass
1½ oz. Kahlua optional
¾ oz. Myers's Jamaican Rum optional
2-3 scoops vanilla ice cream
4 oz. whole milk
⅓ large banana
1 oz. chocolate syrup
2 tbsp. creamy peanut butter
Whipped cream garnish

MERRY WIDOW (1)......*Stir & Strain*
Cocktail glass, chilled
1½ oz. Dubonnet
1½ oz. Dry Vermouth
Dash Angostura bitters
2 dashes Pernod optional
2 dashes Benedictine D.O.M. optional
Lemon twist garnish

MERRY WIDOW (2)......*Shake & Strain*
Collins glass, ice
1½ oz. Gin
1 oz. orange juice
1 oz. sweet 'n' sour
Shake and strain
Fill with club soda

MEXICAN BLACKJACK
............*Stir & Strain*
Presentation shot glass, chilled
½ oz. Cuervo Especial Tequila
½ oz. Black Velvet Canadian
½ oz. Jack Daniel's
½ oz. Triple Sec

MEXICAN COCOA...............*Build*
Coffee mug, heated
¾ oz. Kahlua
¾ oz. Brandy
Fill with hot cocoa
Whipped cream garnish

MEXICAN COFFEE...............*Build*
Coffee mug, heated
¾ oz. Tequila
¾ oz. Kahlua
Fill with hot coffee
Whipped cream garnish optional

MEXICAN FLAG..................*Layer*
Cordial or pousse-café glass
⅓ fill grenadine
⅓ fill Green Creme de Menthe
⅓ fill 151 Rum

MEXICAN GRASSHOPPER
.........*Shake or Blend*
Cocktail or house specialty glass, chilled
½ oz. White Creme de Cacao
½ oz. Green Creme de Menthe
½ oz. Kahlua
2 oz. half & half cream

MEXICAN ITCH....................*Build*
Presentation shot glass, chilled
Salted rim optional
⅓ fill El Tesoro Muy Añejo
⅓ fill Grand Marnier
⅓ fill fresh lime juice
Lime wedge garnish

MEXICAN MONK..................*Build*
Coffee mug, heated
1 oz. Kahlua
1 oz. Frangelico
½ oz. Brown Creme de Cacao
Fill with hot coffee
Whipped cream garnish

MEXICAN RUNNER
.........*Blend with ice*
House specialty glass, ice
½ oz. Tequila
½ oz. Myers's Jamaican Rum
½ oz. Blackberry Brandy
½ oz. Creme de Banana
½ oz. grenadine
½ oz. fresh lime juice
1 oz. sweet 'n' sour
Lime wheel garnish

MEXICAN SIESTA......*Shake & Strain*
Rocks glass, chilled
Salted rim optional
¾ oz. Sauza Conmemorativo Tequila
¾ oz. Grand Marnier
¾ oz. sweet 'n' sour
Lime wedge garnish

MIAMI ICE...............*Shake & Strain*
House specialty glass, ice
½ oz. Gin
½ oz. Vodka
½ oz. Light Rum
½ oz. Peach Schnapps
1 oz. orange juice
1 oz. sweet 'n' sour
Shake and strain
Fill with Seven-up

MIAMI VICE ....*Blend with ice*
House specialty glass, chilled
1¼ oz. Sambista Cachaça
¾ oz. Blue Curaçao
1½ oz. sweet 'n' sour

MIDNIGHT LACE..................*Build*
Coffee mug, heated
1½ oz. B. & B. Liqueur
½ oz. Triple Sec
1 sugar cube
Fill with hot coffee
Lemon twist
Whipped cream garnish optional

MIDNIGHT MADNESS MARGARITA
See
MARGARITA, MIDNIGHT MADNESS

MIDNIGHT MARGARITA
See MARGARITA, BLUE

MIDORABLE...........*Shake & Strain*
Cocktail glass, chilled
1 oz. Midori
¾ oz. Creme de Banana
¼ oz. fresh lime juice
1 oz. sweet 'n' sour

MIDORI DRIVER..................*Build*
Highball glass, ice
1 oz. Midori
Fill with orange juice
Splash club soda

MIDORI PIÑA COLADA
See PIÑA COLADA, MIDORI

MIDORI STINGER...............*Build*
Rocks glass, ice
1 oz. Midori
1 oz. Brandy
½ oz. White Creme de Menthe

MIDWAY RAT (1)......*Shake & Strain*
Presentation shot glass, chilled
½ oz. Bacardi Rum
½ oz. Amaretto di Saronno
½ oz. Tia Maria
½ oz. pineapple juice

MIDWAY RAT (2)..................*Build*
Bucket glass, ice
1 oz. Bacardi Light Rum
¾ oz. Amaretto di Saronno
¾ oz. Tia Maria
4 oz. pineapple juice
Orange slice and cherry garnish

MIKE COLLINS.........*Shake & Strain*
a.k.a. JOE COLLINS
Collins glass, ice
1 oz. Irish Whiskey
2 oz. sweet 'n' sour
Fill with club soda
Orange slice and cherry garnish

MIKHAIL COCKTAIL
.........*Shake & Strain*
House specialty glass, ice
¾ oz. Stolichnaya Vodka
¾ oz. Chambord
1½ oz. sweet 'n' sour
1 oz. orange juice
Shake and strain
Fill with Champagne
Lemon wedge garnish

MILLIONAIRE COCKTAIL
.........*Shake & Strain*
Cocktail glass, chilled
1½ oz. Bourbon
½ oz. Triple Sec
1 oz. sweet 'n' sour
Dash grenadine
1 egg white

MILLIONAIRE'S COFFEE......*Build*
Coffee mug, heated
½ oz. Kahlua
½ oz. Bailey's Irish Cream
½ oz. Frangelico
½ oz. Grand Marnier
Fill with hot coffee
Whipped cream garnish

MIMOSA.............................*Build*
a.k.a. BUCK'S FIZZ
Champagne glass, chilled
½ fill Champagne
½ fill orange juice
Orange wheel garnish

MIND ERASER (1)..................*Build*
Old fashion glass, crushed ice
¾ oz. Vodka
¾ oz. Kahlua
¾ oz. Rumple Minze Schnapps

MIND ERASER (2)..................*Build*
Rocks glass, ice
1½ oz. Vodka
1½ oz. Kahlua
1 oz. club soda (approximately)

MINNEHAHA............*Shake & Strain*
Collins glass, ice
1½ oz. Gin
½ oz. Dry Vermouth
½ oz. Sweet Vermouth
½ oz. Pernod
½ oz. orange juice

MINT JULEP...........................*Build*
Collins or chimney glass, frosted
  Muddle 3 sprigs of mint with
  ½ oz. simple syrup
2-3 oz. Bourbon
Fill with crushed ice
Whole mint leaf garnish

MIST.....................................*Build*
Rocks glass, crushed ice
1½ oz. requested liquor
  poured over crushed ice

MOCHA FRAPPÉ
See FRAPPÉ, MOCHA

MOCHA JAMOCHA...............*Build*
Coffee mug, heated
¾ oz. Myers's Jamaican Rum
½ oz. Myers's Rum Cream
½ oz. Tia Maria
½ oz. Brown Creme de Cacao
Fill with hot coffee
Whipped cream garnish

MOCHA MY EYE......*Blend with ice*
House specialty glass, chilled
1 oz. Kahlua
1 oz. Vodka
1½ oz. Nestle's chocolate syrup
2 scoops vanilla ice cream
2 tbsp. vanilla yogurt
Whipped cream, shaved chocolate
   & chocolate-covered pretzel garnish

MOJITO..............................*Build*
Bucket glass, ice
1½ oz. Bacardi Light Rum
3 oz. fresh lime juice
½ oz. simple syrup
3-4 sprigs fresh mint
Fill with club soda

MOLOTOV'S COCKTAIL.........*Build*
Rocks glass, ice
1½ oz. Vodka
½ oz. Dr. McGillicuddy's Mentholmint

MONKEY GLAND......*Shake & Strain*
Cocktail glass, chilled
1½ oz. Gin
½ oz. Pernod
½ oz. grenadine
1 oz. orange juice

MONKEY JUICE.................*Build*
Rocks glass, ice
1½ oz. Myers's Jamaican Rum
½ oz. Bailey's Irish Cream
½ oz. Creme de Banana

MONK'S COFFEE.................*Build*
Coffee mug, heated
1¼ oz. Benedictine D.O.M.
¾ oz. Grand Marnier
Fill with hot coffee
Whipped cream garnish

MONTE CRISTO SHOOTER......*Build*
Presentation shot glass
⅓ fill Grand Marnier
⅓ fill Kahlua
⅓ fill hot coffee
Whipped cream garnish

MONTEGO BAY.....................*Build*
Coffee mug, heated
½ oz. Tia Maria
½ oz. Myers's Jamaican Rum
½ oz. Creme de Banana
Fill with hot coffee
Whipped cream garnish

MONTMARTE.........*Shake & Strain*
Champagne glass, chilled
1½ oz. Brandy
½ oz. Benedictine D.O.M.
½ oz. sweet 'n' sour
Dash Angostura bitters
Shake and strain
Fill with Champagne
Lemon twist garnish

MOOSEBERRY.........*Shake & Strain*
House specialty glass, ice
¾ oz. Vodka
¾ oz. Amaretto di Saronno
½ fill cranberry juice
½ fill sweet 'n' sour
Shake and strain
Float 1 oz. Grand Marnier

MOOSE MILK......................*Build*
Highball glass, ice
1 oz. Kahlua
Fill with milk

MOP IN A BUCKET...............*Build*
Bucket glass, ice
1 oz. Myers's Jamaican Rum
½ fill orange juice
½ fill pineapple juice

MOSCOW MULE..................*Build*
Highball glass, ice
1 oz. Vodka
Fill with Ginger Beer
Lime wedge garnish

MOSCOW WITCH..................*Build*
Rocks glass, ice
1½ oz. Vodka
¾ oz. Strega
Lemon twist garnish

MOTHER.............................*Build*
a.k.a. DIRTY MOTHER
Rocks glass, ice
1½ oz. Brandy
½ oz. Kahlua

MOTHER LODE.....................*Build*
Rocks glass, ice
1½ oz. Canadian Whisky
½ oz. Peppermint Schnapps

MOTHER MASON'S DELIGHT
.........*Blend with ice*
House specialty glass
¾ oz. Amaretto di Saronno
¾ oz. Brown Creme de Cacao
½ cup strawberries
2 oz. half & half cream
Strawberry garnish

MOUNT FUGI MARGARITA
See MARGARITA, MOUNT FUGI

MOUNT GAY CAFÉ
.........*Shake & Strain*

Cocktail glass, chilled
1 oz. Mount Gay Eclipse Rum
1 oz. Tia Maria
1 oz. Triple Sec

MR. MURPHY........................*Build*
Rocks glass, ice
1½ oz. Irish Mist
¾ oz. Bailey's Irish Cream

MRS. BAILEY'S BUSH............*Build*
Rocks glass, ice
1 oz. Bushmills Irish Whiskey
1 oz. Bailey's Irish Cream

MRS. BAILEY'S FAVOR.........*Build*
Cappuccino cup, heated
½ oz. Irish Whiskey
½ oz. Bailey's Irish Cream
½ oz. Frangelico
Fill with hot espresso coffee
Spoon on frothed milk
Shaved chocolate garnish

MUDDY RIVER
See SOMBRERO

MUDSLIDE (1).....................*Build*
Bucket glass, ice
1½ oz. Vodka
½ oz. Kahlua
½ oz. Bailey's Irish Cream
Fill with cola

MUDSLIDE (2).....................*Build*
Rocks glass, ice
¾ oz. Vodka
¾ oz. Kahlua
¾ oz. Bailey's Irish Cream

MULATA.............................*Build*
Champagne saucer, crushed ice
1½ oz. Bacardi Light Rum
½ oz. Brown Creme de Cacao
1½ oz. fresh lime juice
Lime wheel garnish

MULTIPLE ORGASM
.........*Shake & Strain*

Rocks glass, chilled
1½ oz. Tia Maria
¾ oz. Amaretto di Saronno
½ oz. half & half cream

NAPOLEON..................*Stir & Strain*
Cocktail glass, chilled
1 oz. Bombay Sapphire Gin
1 oz. Dubonnet Rouge
1 oz. Grand Marnier
Orange twist garnish

NAVY GROG............*Shake & Strain*
Collins glass, ice
1½ oz. Myers's Jamaican Rum
¾ oz. Light Rum
¾ oz. Demerara 151
1½ oz. orange juice
1½ oz. pineapple juice
½ oz. Rose's lime juice

NEGRONI..................*Stir & Strain*
Cocktail glass, chilled
¾ oz. Gin
¾ oz. Campari Aperitivo
¾ oz. Sweet Vermouth
Lemon twist garnish

NELSON'S BLOOD (1)............*Build*
Rocks glass, ice
2 oz. Pusser's Naval Rum
2 oz. ginger beer
½ oz. fresh lime juice
Lime wedge garnish

NELSON'S BLOOD (2)............*Build*
Champagne glass, chilled
1½ oz. Tawny Port
Fill with Champagne

NEUTRON BOMB..................*Layer*
Presentation shot glass, chilled
⅓ fill Kahlua
⅓ fill Bailey's Irish Cream
⅓ fill Butterscotch Schnapps

NEW ORLEAN'S FIZZ
.........*Shake or Blend*

Collins or house specialty glass, ice
1 oz. Gin
1 oz. sweet 'n' sour
2 oz. half & half cream
1 egg white
Shake and strain
Splash club soda
Orange slice and cherry garnish

NEW ORLEAN'S JAZZ TIME
.........*Shake & Strain*

Champagne glass, chilled
1½ oz. Light Rum
½ oz. Peach Schnapps
½ oz. orange juice
Dash Rose's lime juice
Shake and strain
Fill with Champagne
Orange twist garnish

NEW ORLEAN'S MANHATTAN
See MANHATTAN, NEW ORLEAN'S

NEW WORLD SANGRIA
(Serves 2)................Punch
.........Shake or Build
Wine goblet or house specialty glass, ice
5 oz. dry red wine
¾ oz. Peach Schnapps
3 oz. Brut Champagne
¾ oz. cranberry juice
1 oz. orange juice
1½ oz. sweet 'n' sour
¾ oz. grenadine
¾ oz. Rose's lime juice
Float ½ oz. Creme de Cassis
Lime, lemon, and orange wheels garnish

NINA'S COFFEE.................*Build*
Coffee mug, heated
¾ oz. Tuaca
¾ oz. Amaretto di Saronno
Fill with hot coffee
*Whipped cream garnish topped with a drizzle
of grenadine and Green Creme de Menthe*

NORTHERN LIGHTS (1).........*Build*
Coffee mug, heated
1 oz. Yukon Jack
¾ oz. Grand Marnier
Fill with hot coffee

NORTHERN LIGHTS (2).........*Build*
Highball glass, ice
1 oz. Yukon Jack
½ oz. Peach Schnapps
½ fill cranberry juice
½ fill orange juice

NO TELL MOTEL.................*Layer*
Presentation shot glass, chilled
½ fill Dr. McGillicuddy's Mentholmint
½ fill Jack Daniel's

NUT N' HOLLI............*Shake & Strain*
Rocks glass, chilled
½ oz. Irish Mist
½ oz. Amaretto di Saronno
½ oz. Bailey's Irish Cream
½ oz. Frangelico

NUTS TO YOU.........*Shake or Blend*
Cocktail or house specialty glass, chilled
¾ oz. Frangelico
¾ oz. White Creme de Cacao
2 oz. half & half cream

NUTTY IRISHMAN...............*Build*
Rocks glass, ice
1½ oz. Bailey's Irish Cream
½ oz. Frangelico

OCEAN BREEZE
See MADRAS

OLD FASHION.....................*Build*
Rocks or old Fashion glass
2-3 dashes Angostura bitters
½ oz. simple syrup
Add ice
1½ oz. Bourbon
Splash club soda
Orange slice and cherry garnish
Note: *Old Fashions may be made with any
requested dark liquor.*

OLD FASHION, MUDDLED......*Build*
Rocks or old Fashion glass
2-3 dashes Angostura bitters
½ oz. simple syrup
Orange slice and cherry
Splash club soda
**Muddle (crush) fruit thoroughly along
with other ingredients before adding ice
and 1½ oz. bourbon.**

OPERA COCKTAIL......*Stir & Strain*
Cocktail glass, chilled
1½ oz. Gin
½ oz. Dubonnet
½ oz. Maraschino Liqueur
Orange twist garnish

ORANGE BLOSSOM (1)
.........Shake & Strain
Cocktail glass, chilled
Sugar rim optional
1 oz. Gin
1½ oz. orange juice
½ oz. simple syrup

ORANGE BLOSSOM (2).........*Build*
a.k.a. LEFT-HANDED SCREWDRIVER
Highball glass, ice
1 oz. Gin
Fill with orange juice

ORANGE CHILLER...............*Build*
Highball glass, ice
1 oz. requested liquor
½ fill orange juice
½ fill cranberry juice
Note: *A vodka Orange Chiller also called a*
MADRAS

ORANGE CRANBERRY TODDY
.........*Simmer & Build*

Coffee mug, heated
1 oz. Grand Marnier
1 oz. Raspberry Schnapps
½ tsp. fine granulated sugar
2 oz. cranberry juice
4 oz. orange juice
Cinnamon stick
Whole clove
Orange slice garnish
Simmer juices & spices in sauce pan.
Pour into heated mugs with liqueurs.
Garnish and serve

ORANGE MARGARITA
See MARGARITA, ORANGE

ORCHARD HAZE.................*Build*
Coffee mug, heated
½ oz. Apple Schnapps
½ oz. Cinnamon Schnapps
½ oz. Light Rum
Fill with hot apple cider
Whipped cream garnish optional

ORGASM (1).......................*Build*
Bucket glass, ice
½ oz. Kahlua
½ oz. Amaretto di Saronno
½ oz. Bailey's Irish Cream
½ fill half & half cream
½ fill club soda

ORGASM (2).......................*Layer*
Presentation shot glass, chilled
½ fill Peppermint Schnapps
½ fill Myers's Rum Cream

ORSINI.....................*Blend with ice*
House specialty glass
1 oz. Gin
¾ oz. Triple Sec
1 oz. sweet 'n' sour
2 oz. orange juice
2 oz. half & half cream

OUTRIGGER............*Shake & Strain*
House specialty glass, chilled
1 oz. Light Rum
½ oz. Amaretto di Saronno
1½ oz. cranberry juice
1½ oz. pineapple juice
Shake and strain
Float ½ oz. Myers's Jamaican Rum
Orange slice and cherry garnish

OYSTER SHOOTER...............*Build*
Presentation shot glass, chilled
1-2 dashes Tabasco sauce
½ tsp. horseradish
2-3 oz. draft beer
1 raw oyster

PACIFIC RIM...........*Shake & Strain*
House specialty glass, chilled
½ oz. Midori
½ oz. Peach Schnapps
½ oz. sweet 'n' sour
1½ oz. orange juice
1½ oz. cranberry juice
Shake and strain
Fill with Champagne
Lemon twist garnish

PADDY.....................*Stir & Strain*
Cocktail glass, chilled or rocks glass, ice
Dash Angostura bitters optional
½ oz. Sweet Vermouth
1½ oz. Irish Whiskey
Cherry garnish

PADDY O'ROCCO..................*Build*
Bucket glass, ice
1½ oz. Irish Mist
½ oz. half & half optional
Fill with orange juice
Float ½ oz. Amaretto di Saronno

PAISLEY
See FRENCH MARTINI,

PANAMA
See RUM ALEXANDER

PANAMA JACK.....................*Build*
Bucket glass, ice
1½ oz. Yukon Jack
½ fill pineapple juice
½ fill cranberry juice
Splash club soda

PANAMA RED.........*Shake & Strain*
Presentation shot glass, chilled
1 oz. Cuervo Especial Tequila
¾ oz. Triple Sec
¼ oz. sweet 'n' sour
¼ oz. grenadine

PANTHER.................*Shake & Strain*
Rocks glass, ice
1½ oz. Tequila
¾ oz. sweet 'n' sour

PARANOIA............................*Build*
Bucket glass, ice
1 oz. Malibu Rum
1 oz. Amaretto di Saronno
½ fill orange juice
½ fill pineapple juice

PARFAIT..................*Blend with ice*
House specialty glass
1½ oz. requested liqueur
1-2 scoops vanilla ice cream
Whipped cream garnish

PARIS BURNING..................*Build*
Brandy snifter, heated
1 oz. V.S. Cognac
1 oz. Chambord

PARISIAN FRAPPÉ
See FRAPPÉ, PARISIAN

PARPLE THUNDER
.........*Shake & Strain*
Bucket glass, ice
1 oz. Bacardi Black Label Rum
1 oz. Bacardi Light Rum
½ oz. Triple Sec
1½ oz. grape juice
1½ oz. cranberry juice
Shake and strain
Splash club soda

PASSION ALEXANDER
.........*Shake or Blend*
Cocktail or House specialty glass, chilled
¾ oz. Opal Nera Sambuca
¾ oz. White Creme de Cacao
1½ oz. half & half cream

PASSIONATE POINT
.........*Shake & Strain*
House specialty glass, ice
¾ oz. Grand Marnier
¾ oz. Mount Gay Eclipse Rum
¾ oz. Peach Schnapps
2 oz. orange juice
2 oz. cranberry juice

PASSIONATE SCREW
.........*Shake & Strain*
Bucket glass, ice
1 oz. Vodka
1 oz. Malibu Rum
1 oz. Chambord
½ oz. grenadine
½ fill orange juice
½ fill pineapple juice
Orange slice and cherry garnish

PASSION POTION......*Shake or Blend*
House specialty glass, chilled
¾ oz. Gin
¾ oz. Vodka
¾ oz. Light Rum
½ oz. grenadine
2½ oz. orange juice
2½ oz. pineapple juice
Shake and strain or blend with ice
Splash Seven-up

PEACH BLASTER..................*Build*
Highball glass, ice
1¼ oz. Peach Schnapps
Fill with cranberry juice

PEACH BREEZE.....................*Build*
Highball glass, ice
1 oz. Peach Schnapps
½ oz. Vodka
½ fill cranberry juice
½ fill grapefruit juice

PEACH DAIQUIRI
See DAIQUIRI, FRUIT

PEACH FUZZ............*Shake & Strain*
Rocks glass, chilled
1¼ oz. Vodka
¾ oz. Peach Schnapps
¼ oz. cranberry juice
¼ oz. orange juice

PEACHIE KEEN.........*Blend with ice*
House specialty glass
1 oz. Peach Schnapps
1 oz. Galliano
1-2 scoops vanilla ice cream
½ oz. half & half cream

PEACH MARGARITA
See MARGARITA, FRUIT

PEARL HARBOR.....................*Build*
Highball glass, ice
1 oz. Midori
½ oz. Vodka
Fill with pineapple juice

PEAR MARGARITA (PEARITA)
See MARGARITA PEAR

PECKERHEAD.........*Shake & Strain*
Rocks glass, chilled
¾ oz. Yukon Jack
¾ oz. Amaretto di Saronno
¾ oz. pineapple juice

PEDRO COLLINS
See COLLINS

PEPPERMINT COOLER.........*Build*
Highball glass, ice
1 oz. Peppermint Schnapps
Fill with Seven-up

PEPPERMINT PATTIE
.........*Shake or Blend*
Cocktail or House specialty glass, chilled
¾ oz. White Creme de Cacao
¾ oz. Peppermint Schnapps
2 oz. half & half cream

PERFECT BRANDY MANHATTAN
See MANHATTAN,
PERFECT BRANDY

PERFECT COCKTAIL
See MARTINI, PERFECT

PERFECT MANHATTAN
See MANHATTAN, PERFECT

PERFECT ROB ROY
See ROB ROY, PERFECT

PERFECT SOUTHERN
COMFORT MANHATTAN
See MANHATTAN, PERFECT
SOUTHERN COMFORT

PERIODISTA...............*Blend with ice*
House specialty glass
1¼ oz. Light Rum
½ oz. Triple Sec
¼ oz. Apricot brandy
½ oz. simple syrup
1 oz. fresh lime juice
Lime wedge garnish

PERSUADER.......................*Build*
Highball glass, ice
½ oz. Amaretto di Saronno
½ oz. Brandy
Fill with orange juice

PETER PRESCRIPTION.........*Build*
Coffee mug, heated
½ oz. Tia Maria
½ oz. Grand Marnier
½ oz. Chambord
¼ oz. Myers's Jamaican Rum
Fill with hot coffee
Whipped cream garnish

PHILIPPI CREEK.................*Build*
Brandy snifter, ice
1 oz. Sambuca
1 oz. V.S. Cognac
4 oz. hot espresso coffee
Splash Bailey's Irish Cream
Lemon twist garnish

PIERRE COLLINS
See COLLINS

PILGRIM.................*Blend with ice*
House specialty glass, chilled
1½ oz. Bacardi Light Rum
½ oz. grenadine
4 oz. cranberry juice
4 oz. orange sherbet

PIMM'S CUP.......................*Build*
Collins glass, ice
1½ oz. Pimm's Cup No. 1
Fill with Seven-up
Cucumber slice and lemon twist garnish

PIÑA COLADA............*Blend with ice*
House specialty glass
1 oz. Light Rum
2 oz. coconut syrup
3 oz. pineapple juice
½ oz. half & half cream optional
Pineapple wedge garnish

PIÑA COLADA, AMARETTO
.........*Blend with ice*
House specialty glass
1 oz. Amaretto di Saronno
1 oz. Light Rum
2 oz. coconut syrup
3 oz. pineapple juice
½ oz. half & half cream optional
Pineapple wedge garnish

PIÑA COLADA, AUSSIE
.........*Blend with ice*
a.k.a. FLYING KANGAROO
House specialty glass
1 oz. Light Rum
½ oz. Galliano
½ oz. Vodka
½ oz. orange juice
2 oz. coconut syrup
3 oz. pineapple juice
½ oz. half & half cream optional
Pineapple wedge garnish

PIÑA COLADA, BAHAMA
.........*Blend with ice*
House specialty glass
1¼ oz. Midori
1 oz. Creme de Banana
1 oz. orange juice
2 oz. coconut syrup
2 oz. pineapple juice
½ oz. half & half cream optional
Pineapple wedge garnish

PIÑA COLADA, BRAZILIAN
.........*Blend with ice*
House specialty glass
1 oz. Sambista Cachaça
1 oz. Light Rum
2 oz. coconut syrup
3 oz. pineapple juice
Fresh fruit garnish

PIÑA COLADA, CACTUS
.........*Blend with ice*
a.k.a. CACTUS COLADA
House specialty glass
1¼ oz. Tequila
¾ oz. Midori
½ oz. grenadine
1 oz. orange juice
1 oz. pineapple juice
2 oz. coconut syrup
Pineapple wedge garnish

PIÑA COLADA, FRUIT
.........*Blend with ice*
House specialty glass
1 oz. Light Rum
2 oz. coconut syrup
3 oz. pineapple juice
½ cup requested fruit
Fresh fruit garnish

PIÑA COLADA, KAHLUA
.........*Blend with ice*
a.k.a. KAHLUA COLADA
House specialty glass
1 oz. Kahlua
1 oz. Light Rum
2 oz. coconut syrup
3 oz. pineapple juice
½ oz. half & half cream optional
Pineapple wedge garnish

PIÑA COLADA, LIQUEUR-FLAVORED
.........*Blend with ice*
House specialty glass
1 oz. Light Rum
1 oz. requested liqueur
2 oz. coconut syrup
3 oz. pineapple juice
½ oz. half & half cream optional
Pineapple wedge garnish

PIÑA COLADA, MIDORI
.........*Blend with ice*
a.k.a. GREEN EYES
House specialty glass
1 oz. Midori
1 oz. Light Rum
2 oz. coconut syrup
3 oz. pineapple juice
½ oz. half & half cream optional
Pineapple wedge garnish

PIÑA COLADA, TOASTED ALMOND
............*Blend with ice*
House specialty glass
½ oz. Kahlua
½ oz. Amaretto di Saronno
1 oz. Light Rum
2 oz. coconut syrup
3 oz. pineapple juice
½ oz. half & half cream optional
Pineapple wedge garnish

PINEAPPLE MARGARITA (PIÑARITA)
See MARGARITA, PINEAPPLE

PINK BABY...............*Stir & Strain*
Cocktail glass, chilled
1½ oz. Absolut Citron
½ oz. Cherry Marnier
½ oz. fresh lemon juice
Lemon twist garnish

PINK CHEVROLET......*Blend with ice*
Champagne glass, chilled
1 oz. Strawberry liqueur
½ oz. sweet 'n' sour
½ cup strawberry puree
Blend with ice
Fill with Champagne
Fresh strawberry garnish

PINK FLAMINGO......*Shake & Strain*
House specialty glass, ice
1½ oz. Wilderberry Schnapps
2 oz. cranberry juice
2 oz. sweet 'n' sour
Shake and strain
Splash club soda

PINK GATOR........................*Build*
Bucket glass, ice
1¼ oz. Bacardi Black Label Rum
½ fill orange juice
½ fill pineapple juice
Float ½ oz. grenadine

PINK GIN....................*Build or Stir*
Cocktail glass, chilled or rocks glass, ice
2 oz. Plymouth Gin
2 dashes Angostura bitters
Stir and strain
Splash water or club soda optional

PINK LADY (1).........*Shake or Blend*
Cocktail or house specialty glass, chilled
1 oz. Gin
1½ oz. half & half cream
½ oz. grenadine

PINK LADY (2).........*Shake & Strain*
Cocktail glass, chilled
1 oz. Gin
1 oz. Apple Jack
1½ oz. sweet 'n' sour
½ oz. grenadine
1 egg white

PINK LEMONADE......*Shake & Strain*
Rocks glass, chilled
1½ oz. Vodka
½ oz. grapefruit juice
½ oz. cranberry juice
½ oz. sweet 'n' sour

PINK MARGARITA
See MARGARITA, PINK

PINK PARADISE......*Shake & Strain*
House specialty glass, ice
1½ oz. Malibu Rum
1 oz. Amaretto di Saronno
3 oz. cranberry juice
1½ oz. pineapple juice
Pineapple wedge and cherry garnish

PINK SILK PANTIES
See SILK PANTIES

PINK SLIPPER............*Blend with ice*
House specialty glass
1½ oz. Light Rum
1½ oz. coconut syrup
½ oz. grenadine
3 oz. pink lemonade concentrate

PINK SQUIRREL......*Shake or Blend*
Cocktail or house specialty glass, chilled
¾ oz. White Creme de Cacao
¾ oz. Creme de Noyaux
2 oz. half & half cream

PINK SUNSET........................*Build*
Bucket glass, ice
1½ oz. Vodka
½ oz. Mandarine Napoleon Liqueur
5 oz. cranberry juice
½ oz. fresh lemon juice
Kiwi slice garnish

PISCO SOUR............*Shake & Strain*
Sour glass, chilled
Sugar rim optional
3 dashes Angostura bitters
1¼ oz. Pisco Brandy
2 oz. sweet 'n' sour
Orange slice and cherry garnish

PITLESS SHOT.....................*Build*
Presentation shot glass, chilled
⅓ fill Peach Schnapps
⅓ fill Vodka
⅓ fill orange juice

PIZZETTI.............................*Build*
Champagne glass, chilled
½ fill with Champagne
¼ fill orange juice
¼ fill grapefruit juice

PLAID COLLINS
See COLLINS

PLAIN ALEXANDER
See GIN ALEXANDER

PLANTER'S PUNCH
.........*Shake & Strain*
Collins glass, ice
1½ oz. Myers's Dark Rum
½ oz. grenadine
2 dashes Angostura bitters
1½ oz. sweet 'n' sour
1½ oz. orange juice
Orange slice and cherry garnish

PLYMOUTH ROCKS...............*Build*
Bucket glass, ice
1½ oz. Bacardi Light Rum
½ fill grape juice
½ fill club soda

POIRE-SUISSE.....................*Build*
Champagne glass, chilled
¾ oz. Poire William Eau de Vie
¾ oz. Chocolate-Suisse
Fill with Champagne

PORT AND LEMON...............*Build*
Wine glass
2 oz. Tawny Port
Fill with Seven-up

PORT IN A STORM......*Stir & Strain*
Wine or Collins glass, ice
2 oz. Port
¾ oz. Brandy
4 oz. dry red wine
Mint sprig garnish

POUSSE CAFÉ (1).................*Layer*
Cordial or pousse café glass, chilled
⅕ fill Grenadine
⅕ fill Green Creme de Menthe
⅕ fill Triple Sec
⅕ fill Sloe Gin
⅕ fill Brandy

POUSSE CAFÉ (2)................*Layer*
Cordial or pousse café glass, chilled
⅙ fill Grenadine
⅙ fill Yellow Chartreuse
⅙ fill White Creme de Menthe
⅙ fill Apricot Brandy
⅙ fill Green Chartreuse
⅙ fill Brandy

POUSSE CAFÉ (3)................*Layer*
Cordial or pousse café glass, chilled
⅐ fill Grenadine
⅐ fill Kahlua
⅐ fill White Creme de Menthe
⅐ fill Blue Curaçao
⅐ fill Galliano
⅐ fill Green Chartreuse
⅐ fill Brandy

POUSSE CAFÉ, FOUR-WAY......*Layer*
Cordial or pousse café glass, chilled
¼ fill Kahlua
¼ fill White Creme de Menthe
¼ fill Galliano
¼ fill Bailey's Irish Cream

POUSSE CAFÉ, TUACA.........*Layer*
Cordial or pousse café glass, chilled
¼ fill grenadine
¼ fill White Creme de Menthe
¼ fill Midori
¼ fill Tuaca

PRAIRIE FIRE........................*Build*
Presentation shot glass
1¼ oz. Gold Tequila
4-5 dashes Tabasco sauce

PRAIRIE OYSTER...............*Build*
Old Fashion glass, NO ice
1½ oz. Brandy optional
1 egg yolk
2 dashes wine vinegar
1 tsp. Worchestershire sauce
1-2 dashes Tabasco sauce
½ tsp. salt
2 oz. tomato juice
Stir gently; do not break egg yolk

PREMIUM WHITE RUSSIAN
See WHITE RUSSIAN, PREMIUM

PRESBYTERIAN....................*Build*
Highball glass, ice
1 oz. requested liquor
½ fill ginger ale
½ fill club soda

PRESIDENTÉ...............*Stir & Strain*
Cocktail glass, chilled
1½ oz. Light Rum
½ oz. Dry Vermouth
½ oz. Triple Sec
Dash grenadine

PROVINCE TOWN
.........*Shake & Strain*
House specialty glass, ice
1 oz. Absolut Vodka
½ oz. Absolut Citron
2 oz. grapefruit juice
2 oz. cranberry juice
Shake and strain
Fill with club soda
Lemon wedge garnish

PUCCINI..............................*Build*
Champagne glass, chilled
½ fill tangerine juice
½ fill Champagne

PURPLE FLIRT.........*Shake & Strain*
Rocks glass, chilled
1 oz. Myers's Jamaican Rum
¼ oz. Blue Curaçao
½ oz. sweet 'n' sour
¼ oz. grenadine
1 oz. pineapple juice

PURPLE GECKO
See MARGARITA, PURPLE

PURPLE HAZE
See ICED TEA, RASPBERRY

PURPLE HOOTERS...............*Build*
Rocks glass, chilled
1 oz. Absolut
1 oz. Chambord
1 oz. sweet 'n' sour
Splash Seven-up

PURPLE KAMI
See KAMIKAZE, PURPLE

PURPLE MARGARITA
See MARGARITA, PURPLE

PURPLE MATADOR
.........*Shake & Strain*
Sherry or pousse café glass, chilled
1½ oz. Amaretto di Saronno
½ oz. Chambord
½ oz. pineapple juice

PURPLE PASSION..................*Build*
Bucket glass, ice
1 oz. Peach Schnapps
⅓ fill orange juice
⅓ fill cranberry juice
⅓ fill pineapple juice
Float ½ oz. Chambord

PUSSER'S PAIN KILLER
.........*Shake or Blend*
House specialty glass, ice
2 oz. Pusser's Naval Rum
1 oz. coconut syrup
1 oz. orange juice
4 oz. pineapple juice
Sprinkle nutmeg garnish

PUSSER'S STALEMATE.........*Build*
Coffee mug, heated
1¼ oz. Pusser's Naval Rum
½ oz. Kahlua
½ oz. Brown Creme de Cacao
Fill with hot chocolate

QUAALUDE............*Shake & Strain*
Rocks glass, chilled
½ oz. Vodka
½ oz. Frangelico
½ oz. Kahlua
½ oz. Brown Creme de Cacao
½ oz. half & half cream

QUAALUDE, ALASKAN.........*Build*
Rocks glass, ice
1½ oz. Attakiska Vodka
½ oz. White Creme de Cacao
½ oz. Frangelico

QUAALUDE, IRANIAN
.........*Shake & Strain*
Old fashion glass, chilled
½ oz. Vodka
½ oz. Kahlua
½ oz. Bailey's Irish Cream
½ oz. Amaretto di Saronno
½ oz. Frangelico

QUAALUDE, RUSSIAN.........*Build*
Rocks glass, ice
½ oz. Stolichnaya Vodka
½ oz. Frangelico
½ oz. Kahlua
½ oz. Bailey's Irish Cream

QUARTER DECK..................*Build*
a.k.a. QUARTERMASTER
Rocks glass, ice
1½ oz. Myers's Jamaican Rum
¾ oz. Sherry
Dash Rose's lime juice
Lime wedge garnish

RAINBOW SHOOTER...........*Layer*
Presentation shot glass, chilled
⅓ fill Creme de Noyaux
⅓ fill Midori
⅓ fill White Creme de Menthe

RAMOS FIZZ............*Shake or Blend*
Collins or house specialty glass, ice
1 oz. Gin
1 oz. sweet 'n' sour
2 oz. half & half cream
1 egg white
½ oz. simple syrup
2 dashes orange flower water
Shake and strain or blend with ice
Splash club soda
Orange twist garnish

RANCHO VALENCIA
RUM PUNCH.........*Shake & Strain*
Wine goblet, ice
1 oz. Bacardi Light Rum
1 oz. Mount Gay Eclipse Rum
1½ oz. pineapple juice
1½ oz. orange juice
1-2 dashes Angostura bitters
Shake and strain
Float ¾ oz. Myers's Jamaican Rum
Orange, lemon, and lime wheels garnish

RASPBERRY GIMLET
See GIMLET, RASPBERRY

RASPBERRY MARGARITA
See MARGARITA, RASPBERRY

RASPBERRY RUM CREAM
............*Blend with ice*
House specialty glass
1 oz. Light Rum
¾ oz. White Creme de Cacao
¾ oz. Chambord
1½ oz. raspberry yogurt
1 scoop raspberry ice cream
2 oz. half & half cream

RASPBERRY TORTE..............*Layer*
Cordial or pousse café glass, chilled
½ fill Chambord
½ fill Vodka

RASTA MAN.......................*Layer*
Presentation shot glass, chilled
⅓ fill Tia Maria
⅓ fill Myers's Rum Cream
⅓ fill Chocolate Schnapps

RASTA SPLEEF.....................*Build*
Bucket glass, ice
1½ oz. Myers's Jamaican Rum
2 oz. orange juice
4 oz. pineapple juice

RAZORBACK HOGCALLER
......................*Build*
Rocks glass, ice
1½ oz. 151 proof Rum
½ oz. Green Chartreuse

RAZZLE DAZZLE..................*Build*
Highball glass, ice
1 oz. Raspberry Schnapps
Fill with cranberry juice
Splash club soda

RECESSION DEPRESSION
............*Stir & Strain*
Cocktail glass, chilled
1½ oz. Absolut Citron
½ oz. Triple Sec
½ oz. fresh lemon juice
2-3 dashes Rose's lime juice
Lime wedge garnish

RED BEER............................*Build*
Beer glass or mug, chilled
Fill with draft beer
Splash of tomato juice or Bloody Mary mix

RED BEER SHOOTER............*Build*
Presentation shot glass, chilled
2-3 dashes Tabasco sauce
½ fill draft beer
½ fill Bloody Mary Mix

RED DEATH........................*Build*
Presentation shot glass, chilled
½ oz. Stolichnaya Vodka
½ oz. Cinnamon Schnapps
½ oz. Yukon Jack
½ oz. 151 proof rum

RED HOT MARGARITA
See MARGARITA, RED HOT

RED LION...............*Shake & Strain*
Cocktail glass, chilled
Sugar rim optional
1 oz. Gin
¾ oz. Grand Marnier
1 oz. sweet 'n' sour
1 oz. orange juice

RED RUSSIAN.....................*Build*
Rocks glass, ice
1½ oz. Vodka
½ oz. Cherry Heering

RED SNAPPER
See GIN MARY

RED WINE COOLER
See WINE COOLER

RED ZIPPER.......................*Build*
Bucket glass, ice
¾ oz. Galliano
¾ oz. Vodka
Fill with cranberry juice

REGGAE WALKER......*Blend with ice*
House specialty glass, chilled
1¼ oz. Peach Schnapps
3 oz. pineapple juice
Blend with ice
Float ¾ oz. Tia Maria
Pineapple wedge garnish

RELEASE VALVE..................*Build*
Highball glass, ice
½ oz. Vodka
½ oz. Light Rum
Fill with pineapple juice
Float ½ oz. grenadine

RESTORATION......*Shake & Strain*
Collins glass, ice
4 oz. dry red wine
¾ oz. Brandy
¾ oz. Chambord
½ oz. sweet 'n' sour
Lemon twist garnish

REVEREND CRAIG
.........*Shake & Strain*
Collins glass, ice
1½ oz. Bourbon
1½ oz. sweet 'n' sour
Shake and strain
Fill with draft beer

REVERSE RUSSIAN..............*Layer*
Cordial or pousse café glass, chilled
½ fill Kahlua
½ fill Vodka

RHETT BUTLER.........*Shake & Strain*
Collins glass, ice
1 oz. Southern Comfort
½ oz. Triple Sec
1½ oz. sweet 'n' sour
½ oz. Rose's lime juice
Shake and strain
Fill with club soda
Lime wedge garnish

RHODODENDRON
............*Blend with ice*
House specialty glass
1½ oz. Light Rum
½ oz. Creme de Noyaux
½ oz. fresh lemon juice
½ oz. fresh lime juice
½ oz. simple syrup
2 oz. pineapple juice

RICKEY..............................*Build*
Highball glass, ice
1 oz. white liquor
Fill with club soda
Lime wedge garnish

RIGOR MORTIS.........*Shake & Strain*
Old fashion glass, chilled
1½ oz. Absolut Vodka
¾ oz. Amaretto di Saronno
1 oz. pineapple juice
1 oz. orange juice

RIO RITA..................*Shake or Blend*
Cocktail or house specialty glass, chilled
1½ oz. Sambista Cachaça
2 oz. sweet 'n' sour
½ oz. simple syrup
Lime wheel garnish

RITZ FIZZ...............*Shake & Strain*
House specialty glass, ice
1 oz. Amaretto di Saronno
½ oz. Blue Curaçao
1½ oz. sweet 'n' sour
Shake and strain
Fill with Champagne
Lemon twist garnish

RITZ PICK-ME-UP
        ....*Shake & Strain*
Champagne glass, chilled
1 oz. V.S. Cognac
1 oz. Cointreau
4 oz. orange juice
Shake and strain
Fill with Champagne

RIVER MADNESS..................*Build*
Bucket glass, ice
1¼ oz. Tequila
1½ oz. sweetened lime juice
Fill with club soda
Lime wedge garnish

RIVER SEINE CAPPUCCINO
        ....*Build*
Cappuccino cup, heated
1 oz. Kahlua
¾ oz. V.S. Cognac
Fill with hot espresso coffee
Spoon on frothed milk
Shaved chocolate garnish

RIVIERA.............................*Build*
Rocks glass, ice
¾ oz. Light Rum
¾ oz. Cointreau
¾ oz. Chambord

ROASTED TOASTED ALMOND
        ....*Shake or Blend*
Cocktail or house specialty glass, chilled
½ oz. Amaretto di Saronno
½ oz. Kahlua
½ oz. Vodka
2 oz. half & half cream

ROB ROY.....................*Build or Stir*
Cocktail glass, chilled or rocks glass, ice
Dash Angostura bitters optional
½ oz. Sweet Vermouth
1½ oz. Scotch
Cherry garnish
Note: **ROB ROY** *is a* **MANHATTAN** *made
with Scotch instead of Bourbon*

ROB ROY, DRY............*Build or Stir*
Cocktail glass, chilled or rocks glass, ice
Dash Angostura bitters optional
¼ oz. Dry Vermouth
1½ oz. Scotch
Olives or lemon twist garnish

ROB ROY, PERFECT......*Build or Stir*
Cocktail glass, chilled or rocks glass, ice
Dash Angostura bitters optional
¼ oz. Dry Vermouth
¼ oz. Sweet Vermouth
1½ oz. Scotch
Lemon twist garnish

ROCKET..............................*Build*
Bucket glass, ice
1½ oz. Yukon Jack
Fill with lemonade
Float ½ oz. 151 Rum

ROCK LOBSTER.........*Blend with ice*
House specialty glass, chilled
1 oz. Malibu Rum
½ oz. Creme de Banana
½ oz. Myers's Jamaican Rum
½ oz. grenadine
1½ oz. orange juice
1½ oz. pineapple juice
Blend with ice
Float ½ oz. Myers's Jamaican Rum
Orange slice and cherry garnish

ROCKS, LIQUOR or LIQUEUR
        ....*Build*
Rocks glass, ice
1½ oz. requested liquor or liqueur
  poured over cubed ice

RODEO DRIVER......*Shake & Strain*
Bucket glass, ice
1½ oz. Gold Tequila
½ oz. Mandarine Napoleon
1½ oz. sweet 'n' sour
1 oz. pineapple juice
Shake and strain
Fill club soda
Orange slice garnish

ROLLS ROYCE............*Stir & Strain*
Cocktail glass, chilled
1 oz. Gin
1 oz. Benedictine D.O.M.
½ oz. Dry Vermouth
½ oz. Sweet Vermouth
Lemon twist garnish

ROOT BEER........................*Build*
Bucket glass, ice
1 oz. Kahlua
¾ oz. Galliano
¾ oz. Vodka
Fill with cola

ROOT BEER FLOAT...............*Build*
Bucket glass, ice
1 oz. Kahlua
¾ oz. Galliano
½ oz. Vodka optional
½ fill cola
½ fill half & half cream

ROOT BEER TOOTER............*Build*
Highball glass, ice
¾ oz. Rootbeer Schnapps
¾ oz. Vodka
¾ oz. half & half cream
Fill with cola

ROOT CANAL.........*Shake & Strain*
House specialty glass, ice
½ oz. Light Rum
½ oz. Gin
½ oz. Vodka
½ fill orange juice
½ fill pineapple juice
Shake and strain
Float ½ oz. Myers's Jamaican Rum
Float ½ oz. grenadine

ROSARITA MARGARITA
See MARGARITA, ROSARITA

ROSÉ COOLER
See WINE COOLER

ROXANNE...............*Shake & Strain*
Presentation shot glass, chilled
¾ oz. Absolut Vodka
¾ oz. Peach Schnapps
½ oz. Amaretto di Saronno
½ oz. orange juice
½ oz. cranberry juice

ROYAL CANADIAN...............*Build*
Presentation shot glass
⅓ fill Kahlua
⅓ fill Amaretto di Saronno
⅓ fill Crown Royal

ROY ROGERS........................*Build*
Bucket or collins glass, ice
Fill with cola
Float 1 oz. grenadine
Cherry garnish

ROYAL FIZZ............*Shake or Blend*
House specialty glass, ice
1 oz. Gin
2 oz. half & half cream
1 egg
1 oz. sweet 'n' sour
½ oz. simple syrup
Shake and strain or blend with ice
Splash club soda

ROYAL STREET COFFEE.........*Build*
Coffee mug, heated
¾ oz. Amaretto di Saronno
¾ oz. Kahlua
½ tsp. nutmeg
Fill with hot coffee
Whipped cream garnish optional

RUBY RED...........................*Build*
Bucket glass, ice
1½ oz. Absolut Citron
Fill with grapefruit juice

RUDDY MIMOSA..................*Build*
Champagne glass, chilled
3 oz. Champagne
1½ oz. orange juice
1½ oz. cranberry juice
½ oz. Peach Schnapps optional

RUM ALEXANDER
.........*Shake or Blend*
a.k.a. PANAMA
Cocktail or house specialty glass
¾ oz. White Creme de Cacao
¾ oz. Light Rum
2 oz. half & half cream
Nutmeg garnish

RUMBA.................*Shake & Strain*
Collins glass, ice
1½ oz. Myers's Jamaican Rum
¾ oz. Light Rum
¾ oz. Gin
1½ oz. sweet 'n' sour
½ oz. grenadine
½ oz. Rose's lime juice

RUMBALL...........................*Build*
Brandy snifter, ice optional
1½ oz. Myers's Jamaican Rum
½ oz. Chocolate Liqueur

RUMPLEMEISTER...............*Build*
a.k.a. SCREAMING NAZI
Presentation shot glass, chilled
1 oz. Rumple Minze Schnapps
1 oz. Jägermeister

RUM RUNNER (1)......*Shake & Strain*
House specialty glass, ice
½ oz. Bacardi Light Rum
½ oz. Myers's Jamaican Rum
½ oz. Creme de Banana
½ oz. Blackberry Brandy
2 oz. sweet 'n' sour
2 oz. orange juice
Shake and strain
Float ½ oz. grenadine

RUM RUNNER (2)......*Shake & Strain*
Rocks glass, chilled
¾ oz. Blackberry Brandy
¾ oz. Creme de Banana
¾ oz. Bacardi Black Label Rum
½ oz. orange juice
½ oz. sweet 'n' sour

RUM SCREW........................*Build*
Highball glass, ice
1 oz. Light Rum
Fill with orange juice

RUN, SKIP AND GO NAKED
.........*Shake & Strain*
House specialty glass, ice
½ oz. Brandy
½ oz. Light Rum
½ oz. Gin
½ oz. Triple Sec
1½ oz. sweet 'n' sour
Shake and strain
Fill with draft beer

RUSSIAN' ABOUT......*Shake & Strain*
Cocktail glass, chilled
1½ oz. Stolichnaya Vodka
½ oz. Bailey's Irish Cream
½ oz. Tia Maria
¼ oz. Frangelico

RUSSIAN BEAR.........*Shake or Blend*
Cocktail or house specialty glass, chilled
1 oz. Kahlua
½ oz. Vodka
1½ oz. half & half cream

RUSSIAN NIGHTS
.........*Shake & Strain*
Champagne glass, chilled
1½ oz. Stolichnaya Limonnaya
1½ oz. orange juice
1½ oz. cranberry juice
Shake and strain
Fill with Champagne
Lemon wheel garnish

RUSSIAN QUAALUDE
See QUAALUDE, RUSSIAN

RUSSIAN SUNRISE...............*Build*
Bucket glass, ice
1 oz. Vodka
Fill with orange juice
Float ½ oz. grenadine

RUSTY NAIL (1).....................*Build*
a.k.a. SCOTCH PLAID
Rocks glass, ice
1½ oz. Scotch
½ oz. Drambuie

RUSTY NAIL (2).....................*Build*
Presentation shot glass
Fill with Bacardi Light Rum
2-3 dashes Tabasco sauce

SACRIFICE FLY.....................*Build*
Coffee mug, heated
½ oz. Brandy
½ oz. Butterscotch Schnapps
½ oz. Chocolate Schnapps
Fill with hot chocolate
Whipped cream garnish

SAINT MORITZ.....................*Layer*
Cordial or sherry glass, chilled
¾ fill Chambord
¼ fill half & half cream

SAKE MARGARITA
See MARGARITA, SAKE

SAKINI (SAKE MARTINI)
See MARTINI, SAKE

SALTY BULL...........................*Build*
Highball glass, salted rim
Add ice
1 oz. Tequila
Fill with grapefruit juice

SALTY DOG........................*Build*
Highball glass, salted rim
Add ice
1 oz. Vodka
Fill with grapefruit juice
Note: *May be requested made with gin*
instead of vodka

SALTY DOGITRON...............*Build*
Highball glass, salted rim
Add ice
1½ oz. Absolut Citron
Dash grenadine
Fill with grapefruit juice

SAMBUCA CON MOSCA
See La MOSCA

SAMBUCA MOCHA FRAPPÉ
See FRAPPÉ, SAMBUCA MOCHA

SAN ANDREAS FAULT.........*Build*
Coffee mug, heated
½ oz. Myers's Jamaican Rum
½ oz. Banana Schnapps
½ oz. Chocolate Schnapps
Fill with hot coffee
Whipped cream garnish

SAND BLASTER..................*Build*
House specialty glass, ice
1½ oz. Jägermeister
¾ oz. C.J.Wray Dry Rum
Fill with cola
Lime wedge garnish

SANGRIA...........................*Build*
Wine glass or goblet, ice
3-4 oz. dry red wine
¾ oz. Peach Schnapps
1½ oz. orange juice
1½ oz. sweet 'n' sour
¾ oz. grenadine
¾ oz. Rose's lime juice
Lime, lemon, and orange wheels garnish

SANTIAGO (1).........*Shake & Strain*
House specialty glass, ice
¾ oz. Bacardi Black Label
½ oz. Myers's Jamaican Rum
½ oz. Triple Sec
½ oz. Rose's lime juice
2 oz. sweet 'n' sour
2 dashes Angostura bitters
Shake and strain
Fill with Champagne
Lime wheel garnish

SANTIAGO (2).........*Shake & Strain*
House specialty glass, ice
1½ oz. Light Rum
¾ oz. Myers's Jamaican Rum
¾ oz. Triple Sec
½ oz. Rose's lime juice
1½ oz. sweet 'n' sour
2 dashes Angostura bitters

SASSAFARAS SUNSET
.........*Shake & Strain*
House specialty glass, ice
1 oz. Malibu Rum
1 oz. Bacardi Black Label Rum
½ oz. Triple Sec
1 oz. sweet 'n' sour
1 oz. orange juice
3 oz. cranberry juice
Shake and strain
Fill with club soda
Orange slice and cherry garnish

SAVANNAH............*Shake & Strain*
Cocktail glass, chilled
1½ oz. Gin
1 oz. orange juice
1 egg white
Dash White Creme de Cacao

SAVOY CHAMPAGNE COCKTAIL
.....................*Build*
Champagne glass, chilled
Angostura bitters saturated sugar cube
½ oz. Grand Marnier
½ oz. V.S. Cognac
Fill with Champagne
Lemon twist garnish

SAY HEY MARSAILLES.........*Build*
Coffee mug, heated
1 oz. Kahlua
1 oz. Chambord
½ oz. Frangelico
¾ oz. half & half cream
Fill with hot coffee
Whipped cream garnish

SAZERAC.............................*Build*
Old Fashion glass or brandy snifter
Swirl ½ oz. Pernod. Discard excess
2 dashes Angostura bitters
2 dashes Peychaud bitters
Add cubed ice
1½ oz. Rye Whiskey
Lemon twist garnish

SCARLETT O'HARA...............*Build*
Highball glass, ice
1½ oz. Southern Comfort
½ oz. Rose's lime juice
Fill with cranberry juice

SCORPION..............*Shake & Strain*
House Specialty glass, ice
1½ oz. Light Rum
1 oz. Brandy
1 oz. Gin
1 oz. Orgeat or Creme de Noyaux
1 oz. White wine
½ oz. Rose's lime juice
1½ oz. orange juice
1½ oz. sweet 'n' sour

SCOTCH COFFEE.................*Build*
Coffee mug, heated
¾ oz. Scotch
¾ oz. Drambuie
Fill with hot coffee

SCOTCH PLAID
See RUSTY NAIL

SCREAMING FUZZY NAVEL
.....................*Build*
Highball glass, ice
1 oz. Peach Schnapps
½ oz. Vodka
Fill with orange juice

SCREAMING NAZI
See RUMPLEMEISTER

SCREAMING ORGASM.........*Build*
House specialty glass, ice
½ oz. Vodka
½ oz. Kahlua
½ oz. Amaretto di Saronno
½ oz. Bailey's Irish Cream
½ fill half & half cream
½ fill club soda

SCREWDRIVER....................*Build*
Highball glass, ice
1 oz. Vodka
Fill with orange juice

SEABREEZE..........................*Build*
Highball glass, ice
1 oz. Vodka
½ fill grapefruit juice
½ fill cranberry juice
Note: *Substitute rum for vodka*
to make a **SUMMER BREEZE**

SEA SIDE LIBERTY
.........*Blend with ice*
House specialty glass
1 oz. Myers's Jamaican Rum
¾ oz. Kahlua
½ oz. half & half cream
1 oz. coconut cream
3 oz. pineapple juice
Pineapple wedge garnish

SEPARATOR (1)....................*Layer*
Cordial or pousse café glass, chilled
⅓ fill Kahlua
⅓ fill half & half cream
⅓ fill Brandy

SEPARATOR (2)....................*Build*
Rocks glass, ice
1 oz. Brandy
1 oz. Kahlua
½ oz. half & half cream

SEVEN & SEVEN.................*Build*
Highball glass, ice
1 oz. Seagram's 7
Fill with Seven-up

1701 FOG.....................*Build or Stir*
Cocktail glass, chilled or rocks glass, ice
1¼ oz. Smirnoff Vodka
1¼ oz. Chambord
1¼ oz. fresh lime juice

SEVENTH AVENUE
.........*Shake or Blend*
Cocktail or house specialty glass, chilled
¾ oz. Amaretto di Saronno
¾ oz. Truffles Chocolate Liqueur
¾ oz. Drambuie
1½ oz. half & half cream

SEVENTH HEAVEN...............*Build*
Highball glass, ice
1 oz. Seagram's 7
½ oz. Amaretto di Saronno
Fill with orange juice

SEVEN TWENTY-SEVEN (727)
.....................*Build*
Rocks glass, ice
½ oz. Stolichnaya Vodka
½ oz. Kahlua
½ oz. Bailey's Irish Cream
½ oz. Grand Marnier

SEX AT THE BEACH
.........*Shake & Strain*
Rocks glass, chilled
½ oz. Vodka
½ oz. Peach Schnapps
½ oz. Apple Schnapps
½ oz. Grand Marnier
½ oz. Southern Comfort
½ oz. cranberry juice
½ oz. orange juice
½ oz. half & half cream

SEX IN THE WOODS
............*Blend with ice*
House specialty glass, chilled
1½ oz. Vodka
¾ oz. Amaretto di Saronno
½ oz. Tia Maria
2½ oz. pineapple juice

SEX ON THE BEACH (1).........*Build*
Highball glass, ice
½ oz. Vodka
½ oz. Chambord
½ oz. Tia Maria
Fill with pineapple juice

SEX ON THE BEACH (2).........*Build*
Highball glass, ice
¾ oz. Midori
¾ oz. Chambord
Fill with pineapple juice

SEX ON THE BEACH (3)
.........*Shake & Strain*
Rocks glass, chilled
1 oz. Southern Comfort
¾ oz. Chambord
1 oz. pineapple juice
1 oz. orange juice

SEX ON THE BEACH (4)
.........*Shake & Strain*
Rocks glass, chilled
¾ oz. Vodka
¾ oz. Chambord
½ oz. Peach Schnapps
¾ oz. sweet 'n' sour
¾ oz. orange juice

SEX ON THE BEACH (5)
.........*Shake & Strain*
Rock glass, chilled
1½ oz. Midori
¾ oz. Chambord
½ oz. sweet 'n' sour

SHANDY GAFF.....................*Build*
Large beer glass or mug
½ fill draft beer
½ fill ginger ale

SHARK ATTACK..................*Build*
Bucket glass, ice
1 oz. Light Rum
Fill with lemonade
Float ½ oz. Blue Curaçao

SHARK BITE.......................*Build*
Highball glass, ice
1 oz. Myers's Jamaican Rum
Fill with orange juice
Float ¾ oz. grenadine
Orange slice garnish
Note: *Immerse orange slice to resemble shark's fin.*

SHARK'S TOOTH
.........*Shake or Blend*
Cocktail or house specialty glass, chilled
½ oz. Light Rum
½ oz. Blue Curaçao
½ oz. White Creme de Cacao
1½ oz. half & half cream

SHILLELAGH.......................*Build*
House specialty glass, chilled
2 oz. Light Rum
1 oz. Green Creme de Menthe
1 oz. fresh lime juice
½ oz. Rose's lime juice
Green cherry garnish

SHIP WRECK......................*Build*
Bucket glass, ice
1 oz. Malibu Rum
½ oz. pineapple juice
Fill with pineapple juice
Pineapple wedge and cherry garnish

SHIRLEY TEMPLE.................*Build*
Bucket or collins glass, ice
Fill with Seven-up
Float 1 oz. grenadine
Cherry garnish

SHOT IN THE DARK...........*Build*
Presentation shot glass
⅓ fill Yukon Jack
⅓ fill Grand Marnier
⅓ fill hot coffee

SIBERIAN.............................*Build*
Rocks glass, ice
1½ oz. Vodka
½ oz. Brandy
½ oz. Kahlua

SICILIAN KISS....................*Build*
Rocks glass, ice
1 oz. Amaretto di Saronno
1 oz. Southern Comfort

SICILIAN SUNRISE...............*Build*
Bucket glass, ice
1 oz. Tequila
Fill with Orange Pelligrino
Float 1 oz. cranberry juice

SIDE CAR (1)............*Shake & Strain*
Cocktail glass, chilled
Sugar rim optional
1 oz. V.S. Cognac
1½ oz. sweet 'n' sour
½ oz. Cointreau

SIDE CAR (2)............*Shake & Strain*
Cocktail glass, chilled
Sugar rim optional
1 oz. Brandy
1½ oz. sweet 'n' sour
½ oz. Triple Sec

SIDE CAR IN BOMBAY
............*Shake & Strain*
Cocktail glass, ice
Sugar rim optional
1¼ oz. Bombay Sapphire Gin
½ oz. Grand Marnier
½ oz. fresh lemon juice

SIDE CAR ROYALE
............*Shake & Strain*
Cocktail glass, chilled
Sugar rim optional
1 oz. V.S. Cognac
½ oz. Cointreau
½ oz. Benedictine D.O.M.
1½ oz. sweet 'n' sour

SILKEN VEIL........................*Build*
Brandy snifter, ice
1½ oz. Vodka
1½ oz. Dubonnet
Lemon twist garnish

SILK PANTIES (1)..................*Build*
a.k.a. WOO-WOO,
PINK SILK PANTIES
Highball glass, ice
1 oz. Peach Schnapps
½ oz. Vodka
Fill with cranberry juice

SILK PANTIES (2)..................*Build*
Rocks glass, ice
1½ oz. Vodka
½ oz. Peach Schnapps

SILVER BULLET....................*Build*
Rocks glass, ice
1½ oz. Tequila
½ oz. White Creme de Menthe

SILVER CLOUD
..........*Shake or Blend*
House specialty glass, chilled
½ oz. Kahlua
½ oz. Amaretto di Saronno
½ oz. Brown Creme de Cacao
½ oz. Vodka optional
1½ oz. half & half cream

SILVER FIZZ............*Shake & Strain*
House specialty glass, chilled
1 oz. Gin
2 oz. half & half cream
1 egg white
1 oz. sweet 'n' sour
½ oz. simple syrup
Shake and strain
Splash club soda

SILVER SHADOW..................*Build*
Coffee mug, heated
1¼ oz. Amaretto di Saronno
Fill hot English breakfast tea
Lemon wedge garnish

SILVER SPIDER............*Stir & Strain*
Rocks glass, chilled
½ oz. Vodka
½ oz. Light Rum
½ oz. Triple Sec
½ oz. White Creme de Menthe

SINGAPORE SLING
..........*Shake & Strain*
House specialty glass, ice
1 oz. Gin
1½ oz. sweet 'n' sour
½ oz. grenadine
Shake and strain
Fill with club soda
Float ½ oz. Cherry Brandy
Orange slice and cherry garnish

SKINNY DIPPING..................*Build*
Tall specialty glass, ice
¾ oz. Vodka
¾ oz. Peach Schnapps
¾ oz. Amaretto di Saronno
½ fill cranberry juice
½ fill orange juice

SKIP AND GO NAKED
..........*Shake & Strain*
Collins glass, ice
1½ oz. Gin
1½ oz. sweet 'n' sour
½ oz. grenadine
Shake and strain
Fill with draft beer
Note: *This may be ordered with vodka instead of gin.*

SKYSCRAPER......................*Build*
Highball glass, ice
1¼ oz. Bourbon
½ oz. Rose's lime juice
2 dashes Angostura bitters
Fill with cranberry juice
Cucumber garnish optional

SLAM DUNK........................*Build*
Bucket glass, ice
1½ oz. Southern Comfort
½ fill cranberry juice
½ fill orange juice

SLIPPED DISK............*Blend with ice*
House specialty glass, chilled
¾ oz. Myers's Jamaican Rum
¾ oz. Captain Morgan's Spiced Rum
½ oz. Amaretto di Saronno
½ oz. Grand Marnier
½ oz. cranberry juice
½ oz. orange juice
½ oz. sweet 'n' sour
½ oz. grenadine
1 oz. coconut syrup
2 oz. pineapple juice
Pineapple wedge garnish

SLIPPERY DICK.........*Shake & Strain*
Presentation shot glass, chilled
1 oz. Peppermint Schnapps
1 oz. Butterscotch Schnapps

SLIPPERY GREEK..................*Layer*
Presentation shot glass, chilled
⅓ fill Ouzo
⅔ fill Bailey's Irish Cream

SLIPPERY NIPPLE..................*Layer*
Presentation shot glass, chilled
½ fill Sambuca
½ fill Bailey's Irish Cream

SLOE COMFORTABLE SCREW
.....................*Build*
Highball glass, ice
½ oz. Sloe Gin
Fill with orange juice
Float ½ oz. Southern Comfort

**SLOE COMFORTABLE SCREW UP
AGAINST THE WALL**............*Build*
Bucket glass, ice
½ oz. Sloe Gin
½ oz. Southern Comfort
Fill with orange juice
Float ½ oz. Galliano

SLOE GIN FIZZ.........*Shake & Strain*
Bucket or collins glass, ice
1 oz. Sloe Gin
2 oz. sweet 'n' sour
Shake and strain
Fill with club soda

SLOE SCREW........................*Build*
aka: COBRA
Highball glass, ice
1 oz. Sloe Gin
Fill with orange juice

SLOE POKE...........................*Build*
Highball glass, ice
1 oz. Sloe Gin
Fill with cola

SMILES FOR MILES...............*Build*
Rocks glass, ice
¾ oz. Canadian Club
¾ oz. Amaretto di Saronno
¾ oz. Peppermint Schnapps

SMITH & KERNS...................*Build*
a.k.a. SMITH & WESSON
Brandy snifter, ice
1½ oz. Kahlua
½ fill half & half cream
½ fill club soda

SMOOTH DRIVER...............*Build*
Highball glass, ice
1 oz. Vodka
Fill with orange juice
Float ½ oz. Triple Sec

SMOOTHY...........................*Build*
Rocks glass, ice
1½ oz. Bourbon
½ oz. White Creme de Menthe

SMURF PISS............*Shake & Strain*
Old fashion glass, chilled
½ oz. Light Rum
½ oz. Blueberry Schnapps
½ oz. Blue Curaçao
1 oz. sweet 'n' sour
1 oz. Seven-up

SNAKE BITE (1)............*Build or Stir*
Cocktail glass, chilled or rocks glass, ice
1½ oz. Yukon Jack
½ oz. Rose's lime juice
Lime wedge garnish

SNAKE BITE (2)............*Build or Stir*
Beer glass, chilled
½ fill draught ale
½ fill hard apple cider

SNAKE BITE (3)......................*Layer*
Presentation shot glass
½ fill White Creme de Cacao
½ fill Southern Comfort

SNEAKY PEACH.........*Blend with ice*
House specialty glass
1½ oz. Peach Schnapps
¾ oz. grenadine
1 oz. sweet 'n' sour
2 oz. orange juice
2 oz. coconut syrup

SNOWBALL............*Shake or Blend*
Cocktail or house specialty glass, chilled
1 oz. Gin
½ oz. Anisette
1½ oz. half & half cream

SNOWSHOE (1)......................*Build*
Rocks glass, ice
1½ oz. Wild Turkey Bourbon
½ oz. Peppermint Schnapps

SNOWSHOE (2)......................*Build*
Rocks glass, ice
1½ oz. Wild Turkey Bourbon
¾ oz. Dr. McGillicuddy's Mentholmint

SOMBRERO...........................*Build*
a.k.a. MUDDY RIVER
Brandy snifter, ice
1½ oz. Kahlua
½ oz. half & half cream

SONORAN MARGARITA
See MARGARITA, SONORAN

SOUR......................*Shake or Blend*
Sour or house specialty glass, chilled
1 oz. requested liquor or liqueur
2 oz. sweet 'n' sour
Orange slice and cherry garnish

SOUTHERN COMFORT
MANHATTAN
See MANHATTAN, SOUTHERN
COMFORT

SOUTHERN SCREW
see COMFORTABLE SCREW

SOUTH OF FRANCE
............*Blend with ice*
House specialty glass
1 oz. Benedictine & Brandy (B & B)
1½ oz. Light Rum
1½ oz. coconut syrup
4 oz. pineapple juice
Pineapple wedge and cherry garnish

SOVEREIGNTY......................*Build*
Cappuccino cup, heated
1 oz. Chambord
½ oz. Tia Maria
½ oz. White Creme de Cacao
Fill with hot espresso coffee
Layer with frothed milk
Sprinkle shaved chocolate garnish

SPANISH COFFEE
See CALYPSO COFFEE

SPANISH FLY (1)......*Shake & Strain*
Bucket glass, ice
1 oz. Vodka
2 oz. sweet 'n' sour
2 oz. pineapple juice
Shake and strain
Float ½ oz. Blue Curaçao

SPANISH FLY (2).................*Build*
Rocks glass, ice
1½ oz. Tequila
½ oz. Amaretto di Saronno

SPANISH MARTINI
See MARTINI, SPANISH

SPATS COLUMBO.................*Build*
House specialty glass, ice
1½ oz. Light Rum
1 oz. Midori
2 oz. orange juice
2 oz. pineapple juice
Float ½ oz. Sloe Gin
Pineapple wedge and cherry garnish

SPEARMINT TEA.................*Build*
Bucket glass, ice
1¼ oz. Spearmint Schnapps
Fill with iced herbal tea
Lemon wedge garnish

SPERM BANK.......................*Layer*
Presentation shot glass, chilled
⅓ fill Bailey's Irish Cream
⅓ fill White Creme de Cacao
⅓ fill Amaretto di Saronno
1 drop grenadine into center with straw

SPIDER CIDER......................*Build*
Bucket glass, ice
1 oz. Apple Schnapps
1 oz. Vodka
½ fill cranberry juice
½ fill orange juice

SPIKE...................................*Build*
Highball glass, ice
1 oz. Tequila
Fill with grapefruit juice

SPILT MILK............*Shake & Strain*
House specialty glass, ice
1 oz. Bailey's Irish Cream
½ oz. Canadian Club
½ oz. Bacardi Light Rum
½ oz. Creme de Noyaux
1½ oz. half & half cream

SPRING BREAK....................*Build*
Bucket glass, ice
1½ oz. Malibu Rum
½ fill cranberry juice
½ fill Seven-up

SPRITZER...........................*Build*
Wine glass or goblet, ice
½ fill White wine
½ fill club soda
Lime or lemon garnish
Note: *May be requested made with red or rose wine.*

SPY'S DEMISE.........*Shake & Strain*
House specialty glass, ice
¾ oz. Vodka
¾ oz. Gin
¾ oz. Sloe Gin
½ oz. Light Rum
½ oz. grenadine
1 oz. sweet 'n' sour
Shake and strain
Fill with Seven-up

STARBOARD TACK..............*Build*
House specialty glass, ice
1½ oz. Malibu Rum
½ oz. Captain Morgan's Spiced Rum
½ fill cranberry juice
½ fill orange juice
Orange slice and cherry garnish

STARLIGHT...............*Stir & Strain*
Cocktail glass, chilled
2 oz. Vodka
½ oz. Opal Nera Sambuca
Lemon twist garnish

STARS & STRIPES..............*Layer*
Cordial or pousse café glass, chilled
⅓ fill Blue Curaçao
⅓ fill grenadine
⅓ fill half & half cream

STEALTH BOMBER
.........*Shake & Strain*
Bucket glass, ice
1¼ oz. Myers's Jamaican Rum
½ oz. Triple Sec
1½ oz. grapefruit juice
1½ oz. cranberry juice
Shake and strain
Splash club soda optional

STEEPLE JACK.........*Shake & Strain*
Collins glass, ice
1½ oz. Apple Brandy
2½ oz. apple juice
½ oz. Rose's lime juice
Shake and strain
Fill with club soda
Lime wedge garnish

STIFF DICK..............*Shake & Strain*
Presentation shot glass, chilled
1 oz. Bailey's Irish Cream
1 oz. Butterscotch Schnapps

STILLETTO...............*Shake & Strain*
House specialty glass
1 oz. Amaretto di Saronno
¾ oz. Creme de Banana
½ fill orange juice
½ fill pineapple juice

STINGER...........................*Build*
Rocks glass, ice
1½ oz. Brandy
½ oz. White Creme de Menthe

STOCKMARKET ZOO
.........*Shake & Strain*
Bucket glass, ice
½ oz. Tequila
½ oz. Gin
½ oz. Light Rum
½ oz. Bourbon
½ oz. grenadine
2 oz. pineapple juice
1 oz. orange juice

STONE SOUR............*Shake or Blend*
Sour, or house specialty glass, chilled
1 oz. requested liquor or liqueur
1 oz. sweet 'n' sour
1 oz. orange juice
Orange slice and cherry garnish

STRAIGHT SHOOTER............*Build*
Presentation shot glass, chilled
⅓ fill Midori
⅓ fill Vodka
⅓ fill orange juice

STRAWBERRIES 'N' CREAM
............*Blend with ice*
a.k.a. WIMBLETON
House specialty glass
1½ oz. Strawberry Schnapps
½ oz. simple syrup
2 oz. half & half cream
½ cup strawberries
Strawberry garnish

STRAWBERRY ALEXANDRA
.........Blend with ice
House specialty glass, chilled
1 oz. Brandy
1 oz. White Creme de Cacao
5 oz. strawberry puree
1-2 scoops vanilla ice cream
Whipped cream and shaved chocolate garnish

STRAWBERRY BANANA SPLIT
.........Blend with ice
House specialty glass, chilled
¾ oz. Creme de Banana
¾ oz. Myers's Jamaican Rum
½ cup strawberries
1 oz. half & half cream
½ tsp. vanilla
Whipped cream and slice of banana garnish

STRAWBERRY DAIQUIRI
See DAIQUIRI, FRUIT

STRAWBERRY MARGARITA
See MARGARITA, FRUIT

STRAWBERRY MARTINI
See MARTINI, STRAWBERRY

STRAWBERRY NUT
.........Blend with ice
House specialty glass, chilled
1 oz. Frangelico
½ oz. half & half cream
½ cup strawberries
1-2 scoops macadamia ice cream

STRAWBERRY SHAKE
.........Blend with ice
House specialty glass, chilled
1½ oz. Amaretto di Saronno
½ cup strawberries
1-2 scoops vanilla ice cream
1½ oz. half & half cream
Strawberry garnish

STRAWMARETTO COLADA
.........Blend with ice
House specialty glass, chilled
1 oz. Light Rum
1 oz. Amaretto di Saronno
2 oz. coconut syrup
3 oz. pineapple juice
½ cup strawberries
½ oz. half & half cream optional
Strawberry garnish

STUBB'S AYERS ROCK
.........Shake & Strain
House specialty glass, chilled
1½ oz. Stubb's Queensland Rum
2 oz. sweet 'n' sour
3 oz. cranberry juice

SUFFERING BASTARD
.........Shake & Strain
House specialty glass, ice
¾ oz. Bacardi Light Rum
1½ oz. St. James Martinique Rhum
½ oz. Creme de Noyaux
½ oz. Triple Sec
1½ oz. fresh lime juice
½ oz. simple syrup
Cucumber peel garnish

SUISSESSE..............*Shake & Strain*
Collins glass, ice
1 oz. Pernod
2 oz. sweet 'n' sour
Shake and strain
Fill with club soda

SUMMER BREEZE
See SEABREEZE

SUN BURN...........................*Build*
Highball glass, ice
1 oz. Tequila
½ oz. Triple Sec
Fill with cranberry juice
Note: Add splash of pineapple juice to make a
HAWAIIAN SUNBURN

SUNBURNT SEÑORITA
.........Shake & Strain
Cocktail glass, chilled
1¼ oz. El Tesoro Muy Añejo Tequila
1 oz. fresh lime juice
¾ oz. watermelon juice
Lime wedge garnish

SUNSTROKE............*Shake & Strain*
Cocktail glass, chilled
1 oz. Absolut Vodka
½ oz. Grand Marnier
2 oz. grapefruit juice

SUNTAN TEASER......*Shake & Strain*
Rocks glass, chilled
1½ oz. Malibu Rum
½ oz. Maui Schnapps
¼ oz. Triple Sec
¼ oz. Captain Morgan's Spiced rum
½ oz. pineapple juice
Dash grenadine

SURF SIDER...........*Shake & Strain*
Cocktail or house specialty glass, chilled
1¼ oz. Light Rum
½ oz. Blue Curaçao
1¼ oz. pineapple juice
Pineapple, lime and cherry garnish

SUSIE TAYLOR......................*Build*
Highball glass, ice
1 oz. Light Rum
Fill with ginger ale
Lemon wedge garnish
Note: See also **MAMIE TAYLOR**

SWAMPWATER......................*Build*
Mason Jar, ice
1½ oz. Green Chartreuse
Fill with grapefruit juice

SWEET TART (1).........*Blend with ice*
House specialty glass
1½ oz. Vodka
3 oz. cranberry juice
3 oz. pineapple juice
¼ oz. Rose's lime juice
Lime wheel garnish

SWEET TART (2).........*Shake & Strain*
Bucket glass, ice
1¼ oz. Vodka
¾ oz. Chambord
3 oz. sweet 'n' sour
¼ oz. simple syrup optional
Shake and strain
Fill with Seven-up

SWIMMING ASHORE FOR THE
SONGS OF SUNRISE............*Build*
Bucket glass, ice
1½ oz. Bacardi Black Label rum
½ oz. Triple Sec
3 oz. grapefruit juice
½ oz. orange juice
¼ oz. grenadine

TAHITIAN APPLE..................*Build*
Highball glass, ice
1 oz. Light Rum
Fill with apple juice

TAKE THE 'A' TRAIN
.........*Shake & Strain*
House specialty glass, ice
1¼ oz. Absolut Citron
½ oz. Absolut Vodka
2 oz. grapefruit juice
2 oz. cranberry juice
Shake and strain
Fill with club soda
Lemon wedge garnish

TAM-O'-SHANTER...............*Build*
Rocks glass, ice
1½ oz. Kahlua
½ oz. Irish Whiskey
½ oz. half & half cream

TARNISHED BULLET............*Build*
Rocks glass, ice
1½ oz. Tequila
½ oz. Green Creme de Menthe

T-BIRD.....................*Shake & Strain*
Presentation shot glass, chilled
½ oz. Stolichnaya Vodka
½ oz. Grand Marnier
½ oz. Amaretto di Saronno
1½ oz. pineapple juice

TENDER MERCIES..................*Build*
Coffee mug, heated
½ oz. Tuaca
½ oz. Tia Maria
½ oz. Bailey's Irish Cream
Fill with hot coffee
Whipped cream garnish

TENNESSEE MUD........................*Build*
Coffee mug, heated
¾ oz. Jack Daniel's
¾ oz. Amaretto di Saronno
Fill with hot coffee
Whipped cream garnish

TENNESSEE TEA..................*Build*
Highball glass, ice
1 oz. Jack Daniels
½ oz. Brown Creme de Cacao
Fill with cranberry juice
Lemon twist garnish

TEQUADOR.......................*Build*
Bucket glass, ice
1½ oz. Tequila
½ oz. Rose's lime juice
½ oz. grenadine
Fill with pineapple juice

TEQUILA DRIVER..................*Build*
Highball glass, ice
1 oz. Tequila
Fill with orange juice

TEQUILA MARIA
.........*Blend with ice*
House specialty glass, chilled
¾ oz. Tequila
¾ oz. Bacardi Dark Rum
½ oz. Creme de Banana
½ oz. Blackberry brandy
¾ oz. grenadine
1½ oz. sweet 'n' sour
1½ oz. fresh lime juice
½ cup strawberries

TEQUILA MOCKINGBIRD (1)
.........*Shake & Strain*
Cocktail glass, chilled
1½ oz. Tequila
½ oz. Green Creme de Menthe
1½ oz. fresh lime juice
Lime wedge garnish

TEQUILA MOCKINGBIRD (2)
.........*Shake & Strain*
House specialty glass, chilled
1¼ oz. Tequila
¾ oz. Blue Curaçao
2 oz. orange juice
2 oz. sweet 'n' sour
Lime wedge garnish

TEQUILA ROSE....................*Build*
Bucket glass, ice
1½ oz. Tequila
½ oz. Rose's lime juice
Fill with grapefruit juice
Float ½ oz. grenadine

TEQUILA SLAMMER/POPPER
.....................*Build*
Presentation shot glass
½ fill Gold Tequila
½ fill ginger ale
Place napkin and palm over glass, slam glass down on bar top. Drink while foaming

TEQUILA SLIDER.................*Build*
Old fashion glass, chilled
1½ oz. Tequila
2 dashes soy sauce
2 dashes Tabasco sauce
½ tsp. horseradish
½ oz. fresh lime juice
1 medium raw oyster
½ tsp. caviar

TEQUILA QUENCHER...........*Build*
Highball glass, ice
1 oz. Tequila
½ fill orange juice
½ fill club soda
Lime wedge garnish

TEQUILA SUNRISE...............*Build*
Bucket glass, ice
1 oz. Tequila
Fill with orange juice
Float ½ oz. grenadine

TEQUILA SUNSET.................*Build*
Bucket glass, ice
1 oz. Tequila
Fill with orange juice
Float ½ oz. Blackberry Brandy

TEST-TUBE BABY (1)...............*Build*
Presentation shot glass, chilled
½ fill Amaretto di Saronno
½ fill Tequila
Add 2 drops half & half cream

TEST-TUBE BABY (2)...............*Build*
Rocks glass, chilled
¾ oz. Amaretto di Saronno
½ oz. Southern Comfort
2-3 drops Bailey's Irish Cream into center with straw

TEXAS ICED TEA
see ICED TEA, LONG ISLAND

TEXAS TEA (1).......................*Build*
Bucket glass, ice
1½ oz. Chambord
½ oz. Vodka
Fill with pineapple juice

TEXAS TEA (2)............*Shake & Strain*
House specialty glass, ice
¾ oz. Light Rum
¾ oz. Vodka
½ oz. Gin
½ oz. Triple Sec
2 oz. cranberry juice
1½ oz. pineapple juice
1½ oz. orange juice

38TH PARALLEL.....................*Build*
Coffee mug, heated
¾ oz. Chambord
½ oz. Bailey's Irish Cream
½ oz. Brown Creme de Cacao
½ oz. Brandy
Fill with hot coffee
Whipped cream garnish

THUMPER...........................*Build*
Rocks glass, ice
1½ oz. Brandy
½ oz. Tuaca
Lemon twist garnish

TIAJUANA BULLDOG............*Build*
Bucket glass, ice
1 oz. Tequila
¾ oz. Kahlua
2½ oz. milk
Fill with cola

TIAJUANA SCREW..................*Build*
a.k.a. TIAJUANA SPLIT
Highball glass, ice
1 oz. Tequila
½ fill grapefruit juice
½ fill orange juice

TIAJUANA SUNRISE............*Build*
Bucket glass, ice
1 oz. Tequila
Fill with orange juice
5-6 dashes Angostura bitters

TIDAL WAVE (1)......*Shake & Strain*
Rocks glass, chilled
½ oz. Vodka
½ oz. 151 proof Rum
½ oz. Captain Morgan's Spiced Rum
½ oz. cranberry juice
½ oz. sweet 'n' sour

TIDAL WAVE (2)......*Shake & Strain*
Bucket glass, ice
½ oz. Light Rum
½ oz. Captain Morgan's Spiced Rum
½ oz. Malibu Rum
½ oz. Creme de Banana
2 oz. orange juice
Shake and strain
Float ½ oz. Galliano

TIDY BOWL............*Shake & Strain*
Rocks glass, chilled
1½ oz. Stolichnaya Vodka
½ oz. Blue Curaçao
½ oz. sweet 'n' sour

TIGHTER CIDER.................*Build*
Coffee mug, heated
1 oz. Myers's Jamaican Rum
½ oz. Calvados
½ oz. Apple Schnapps
1 tsp. apple butter
2 pinches cinnamon
Fill with hot apple cider
Apple slice garnish

TIGHT SWEATER.................*Build*
Coffee mug, heated
½ oz. Frangelico
½ oz. Kahlua
½ oz. Amaretto di Saronno
½ oz. Bailey's Irish Cream
Fill with hot coffee
Whipped cream garnish

TIP-TOP PUNCH
........*Shake & Strain*
Collins glass, ice
1½ oz. Brandy
½ oz. Benedictine D.O.M.
1½ oz. sweet 'n' sour
½ oz. simple syrup
Shake and strain
Fill with Champagne

T.K.O. ....*Build*
Rocks glass, ice
¾ oz. Tequila
¾ oz. Kahlua
¾ oz. Ouzo

T. 'N' T. ....*Build*
Highball glass, ice
1 oz. Tanqueray Gin
Fill with tonic water
Lime wedge garnish

TOASTED ALMOND
.........*Shake or Blend*
Cocktail or house specialty glass, chilled
¾ oz. Amaretto di Saronno
¾ oz. Kahlua
2 oz. half & half cream

TOASTED ALMOND CAFÉ
....................*Build*
Coffee mug, heated
¾ oz. Amaretto di Saronno
¾ oz. Kahlua
Fill with hot coffee
Whipped cream garnish

TOASTED ALMOND PIÑA COLADA
See PIÑA COLADA, TOASTED
ALMOND

TOBOGGAN TRUFFLE............*Build*
Coffee mug, heated
1 oz. Dr. McGillicuddy's Mentholmint
1 oz. Truffles Chocolate Liqueur
Fill with hot coffee
Whipped cream garnish

TOM BOY
See RED BEER

TOM COLLINS.........*Shake & Strain*
a.k.a. GIN FIZZ
Collins glass, ice
1 oz. Gin
2 oz. sweet 'n' sour
Shake and strain
Fill with club soda
Orange slice and cherry garnish

TOM & JERRY........................*Build*
Coffee mug, heated
1 oz. Light Rum
1 oz. Brandy
1 heaping tbsp. Tom & Jerry batter
Fill with hot milk
Nutmeg garnish

TOM & JERRY BATTER:
Beat together:
12 egg yolks
6 tbsp. sugar
½ tsp. cinnamon,
¼ tsp. clove
Fold 12 beaten egg whites into above mixture

TOM MIX HIGH.....................*Build*
Highball glass, ice
1 oz. Seagram's 7
Dash Angostura bitters
Dash grenadine
Fill with club soda

TOOL.....................................*Build*
Bucket glass, ice
1 oz. Tequila
Fill with orange juice
Float ½ oz. Southern Comfort

TOOTSIE ROLL.....................*Build*
Highball glass, ice
1 oz. Brown Creme de Cacao
½ oz. Vodka
Fill with orange juice

TOP HAT..............................*Build*
Rocks glass, ice
1 oz. Grand Marnier
1 oz. Cherry Marnier

TOREADOR............*Shake or Blend*
Cocktail or house specialty glass, chilled
¾ oz. Tequila
¾ oz. White Creme de Menthe
2 oz. half & half cream

TORONTO.................*Build or Stir*
Cocktail glass, chilled or rocks glass, ice
2 dashes simple syrup
1 dash Angostura bitters
¾ oz. Fernet Branca
1½ oz. Canadian Whisky
Orange twist garnish

TORQUE WRENCH..............*Build*
Presentation shot glass, chilled
⅓ fill Midori
⅓ fill Champagne
⅓ fill orange juice

TOUR de PANAMA
...........*Shake & Strain*
House specialty glass, ice
½ oz. Bacardi Black Label
½ oz. Creme de Banana
2 oz. pineapple juice
2 oz. orange juice
Shake and strain
Float ½ oz. Myers's Jamaican Rum
Float ½ oz. Tia Maria
Orange slice and cherry garnish

TOVARICH..................*Build or Stir*
Cocktail glass, chilled or rocks glass, ice
1½ oz. Vodka
½ oz. Kümmel
½ oz. Rose's lime juice
Lime wedge garnish

TRADE DEFICIT.....................*Build*
Coffee mug, heated
¾ oz. Bailey's Irish Cream
¾ oz. Coffee Schnapps
¾ oz. Peppermint Schnapps
¾ oz. Chocolate Schnapps
Fill with hot coffee
Whipped cream garnish

TRADEWINDS.....................*Build*
Highball glass, ice
1 oz. Mohala Mango Liqueur
½ fill cranberry juice
½ fill grapefruit juice

TRAFFIC LIGHT (1)...............*Layer*
Cordial or presentation shot glass, chilled
⅓ fill Green Creme de Menthe
⅓ fill Creme de Banana
⅓ fill Sloe Gin

TRAFFIC LIGHT (2)...............*Layer*
Cordial or pousse café, chilled
⅓ fill Creme de Noyaux
⅓ fill Galliano
⅓ fill Midori

TRINITY.....................*Build or Stir*
Cocktail glass, chilled or rocks glass, ice
½ oz. Dry Vermouth
1½ oz. Bourbon
Dash Angostura bitters
Dash White Creme de Menthe
Lemon twist garnish

TROPHY ROOM.....................*Build*
Coffee mug, heated
½ oz. Amaretto di Saronno
½ oz. Vandermint
½ oz. Myers's Jamaican Rum
Fill with hot coffee
Whipped cream garnish with
  ½ oz. drizzle of Tia Maria

TROPICAL GOLD...............*Build*
Highball glass, ice
1 oz. Light Rum
½ oz. Creme de Banana
Fill with orange juice

TROPICAL HOOTER...........*Build*
Bucket glass, ice
1½ oz. Malibu Rum
½ oz. Midori
½ fill cranberry juice
½ fill pineapple juice

TROPICAL HUT.........*Shake & Strain*
House specialty glass, ice
1 oz. Midori
1 oz. Light Rum
½ oz. Orgeat
1½ oz. sweet 'n' sour
Pineapple wedge and cherry garnish

TROPICAL MOON
.........*Blend with ice*
House specialty glass
1½ oz. Myers's Jamaican Rum
¾ oz. Amaretto di Saronno
2 oz. coconut syrup
3 oz. pineapple juice
½ oz. half & half cream optional
Pineapple wedge garnish

TROPICAL SPECIAL
.........*Shake & Strain*
House specialty glass, ice
1½ oz. Gin
½ oz. Triple Sec
1 oz. orange juice
1 oz. Rose's lime juice
2 oz. grapefruit juice
Orange slice and cherry garnish

TRYST & SHOUT
.........*Shake & Strain*
Champagne glass, chilled
1½ oz. Amaretto di Saronno
2 oz. sweet 'n' sour
Shake and strain
Fill with Champagne
Lemon twist garnish

TUACA GIMLET
See GIMLET, TUACA

TUACA MARGARITA
See MARGARITA, TUACA

TUACA POUSSE CAFÉ
See POUSSE CAFÉ, TUACA

TURKEY SHOOTER...............*Layer*
Presentation shot glass, chilled
½ fill Peppermint Schnapps
½ fill Wild Turkey Bourbon

TWISTER...................*Shake & Strain*
House specialty glass, ice
1½ oz. Light Rum
¾ oz. Peach Schnapps
¾ oz. Maui Tropical Schnapps
¾ oz. Malibu Rum
3 oz. orange juice
2 oz. pineapple juice
1 oz. cranberry juice

UGLY DUCKLING.................*Build*
Brandy snifter, ice
1½ oz. Amaretto di Saronno
½ fill half & half cream
½ fill club soda

UPTOWN...................*Shake & Strain*
Cocktail glass, chilled
1½ oz. Myers's Jamaican Rum
½ oz. Rose's lime juice
½ oz. orange juice
½ oz. pineapple juice
Dash Triple Sec
Dash Angostura bitters
Dash grenadine

VANDERBILT COCKTAIL
.........*Shake & Strain*
Cocktail glass, chilled
1½ oz. Brandy
¾ oz. Cherry Brandy
2 dashes simple syrup
2 dashes Angostura bitters

VELVET HAMMER
.........*Shake or Blend*
Cocktail or house specialty glass, chilled
¾ oz. Triple Sec
¾ oz. White Creme de Cacao
2 oz. half & half cream

VERMOUTH CASSIS
............*Build or Stir*
Cocktail glass, chilled or brandy snifter, ice
1 oz. Creme de Cassis
1 oz. Dry Vermouth
Lemon twist garnish

VINTNER'S MARGARITA
See MARGARITA, VINTNER'S

VIRGIN BLOODY MARY
See BLOODY MARY, VIRGIN

VIRGIN MARGARITA
See MARGARITA, VIRGIN

VODKA COLLINS
................*Shake & Strain*
Collins glass, ice
1 oz. Vodka
2 oz. sweet 'n' sour
Shake and strain
Fill with club soda
Orange slice and cherry garnish
Note: *Refer to* **COLLINS** *for other recipes in this family.*

VODKA GIBSON
See GIBSON, VODKA

VODKA GIMLET
See GIMLET, VODKA

VODKA GRAND.........*Build or Stir*
Cocktail glass, chilled or rocks glass, ice
1½ oz. Vodka
½ oz. Grand Marnier
½ oz. Rose's lime juice
Orange slice garnish

VODKA MARTINI
See MARTINI, VODKA

VODKA SONIC......................*Build*
Highball glass, ice
1 oz. Vodka
½ fill club soda
½ fill tonic water
Lime wedge garnish

VOODOO MOONDANCE
................*Shake & Strain*
House specialty glass, ice
1½ oz. Myers's Jamaican Rum
1 oz. Bacardi Light Rum
¾ oz. grenadine
1½ oz. pineapple juice
1½ oz. orange juice
1½ oz. grapefruit juice
Shake and strain
Splash club soda
Float ½ oz. Stubb's Queensland Rum
Orange slice and cherry garnish

VOODOO SHOOTER............*Layer*
Presentation shot glass, chilled
⅓ fill Tia Maria
⅓ fill Bailey's Irish Cream
⅓ fill Myers's Jamaican Rum

VULCAN.............................*Build*
Bucket glass, ice
½ oz. Gin
½ oz. Vodka
½ oz. Southern Comfort
½ oz. Malibu Rum
½ fill grapefruit juice
½ fill Seven-up

WADKIN'S GLEN......*Shake & Strain*
Bucket glass, ice
1 oz. Absolut Vodka
½ oz. Creme de Banana
½ oz. Chambord
½ oz. pineapple juice
½ oz. cranberry juice
½ oz. orange juice
Lime wedge garnish

WAIST COAT POCKET
................*Blend with ice*
House specialty glass, chilled
½ oz. Kahlua
½ oz. Amaretto di Saronno
½ oz. Chocolate Schnapps
1-2 scoops vanilla ice cream
½ oz. half & half cream

WALL STREET WIZARD.........*Build*
Rocks glass, ice
½ oz. Gin
½ oz. Vodka
½ oz. Light Rum
½ oz. Blue Curaçao
½ oz. Midori

WANDERER............*Shake & Strain*
Bucket glass, ice
1 oz. Vodka
½ oz. Chambord
½ oz. Wilderberry Schnapps
½ oz. Blue Curaçao
1½ oz. pineapple juice
1½ oz. cranberry juice

WANNA PROBE YA...............*Build*
Bucket glass, ice
1 oz. Captain Morgan's Spiced Rum
¾ oz. Malibu Rum
½ fill cranberry juice
½ fill pineapple juice

WARD EIGHT............*Shake & Strain*
Cocktail glass, chilled
1½ oz. Bourbon
1½ oz. sweet 'n' sour
½ oz. grenadine

WATERGATE.......................*Layer*
Presentation shot glass, chilled
¼ fill Kahlua
¼ fill Myers's Rum Cream
¼ fill Peppermint Schnapps
¼ fill Grand Marnier

WATERMELON (1)..................*Build*
Rocks glass, ice
¾ oz. Southern Comfort
¾ oz. orange juice
¾ oz. Amaretto di Saronno

WATERMELON (2)..................*Build*
Presentation shot glass, chilled
⅓ fill Vodka
⅓ fill Midori
⅓ fill Bailey's Irish Cream
3-5 drops grenadine

WATERMELON (3)..................*Build*
Presentation shot glass, chilled
⅓ fill Vodka
⅓ fill Sloe Gin
⅓ fill orange juice

WATERMELON (4)..................*Build*
Bucket glass, ice
1 oz. Southern Comfort
½ oz. Midori
2 oz. orange juice
Dash grenadine

WATERMELON (5)......*Shake & Strain*
Rocks glass, chilled
1 oz. Southern Comfort
¾ oz. Vodka
¼ oz. grenadine
2 oz. pineapple juice

WEEKEND AT THE BEACH (1)
.....................*Build*
Presentation shot glass, chilled
¾ oz. Apple Schnapps
¾ oz. Peach Schnapps
Splash orange juice
Splash cranberry juice

WEEKEND AT THE BEACH (2)
.........*Shake & Strain*
Old fashion glass, chilled
1 oz. Light Rum
1 oz. Peach Schnapps
1 oz. orange juice
1 oz. pineapple juice

WEEK ON THE BEACH
.........*Shake & Strain*
Presentation shot glass, chilled
¾ oz. Peach Schnapps
¾ oz. Apple Schnapps
½ oz. orange juice
½ oz. pineapple juice
½ oz. cranberry juice

WET DREAM...........*Shake & Strain*
Rocks glass, chilled
¾ oz. Chambord
¾ oz. Creme de Banana
½ oz. orange juice
½ oz. half & half cream

WHALE'S TAIL.........*Blend with ice*
House specialty glass
1 oz. Vodka
1 oz. Captain Morgan's Spiced Rum
¾ oz. Blue Curaçao
1½ oz. sweet 'n' sour
3 oz. pineapple juice
Pineapple wedge garnish

WHAT CRISIS?.........*Shake & Strain*
Presentation shot glass, chilled
½ oz. Peach Schnapps
½ oz. Midori
½ oz. orange juice
½ oz. cranberry juice

WHEN HELL FREEZES OVER
.........*Blend with ice*
House specialty glass
¾ oz. Cinnamon Schnapps
¾ oz. Creme de Banana
2 oz. orange juice
2 oz. cranberry juice

WHIP...........................*Stir & Strain*
Cocktail glass, chilled
¾ oz. Pernod
¾ oz. Brandy
¾ oz. Triple Sec
¾ oz. Dry Vermouth

WHISKY-ALL-IN..................*Build*
Coffee mug, heated
1½ oz. Scotch
1 tsp. sugar
¼ oz. fresh lemon juice
3 oz. hot water
Lemon wedge garnish

WHISKEY SOUR
see SOUR

WHISPER.............................*Build*
Brandy snifter, ice
1 oz. Amaretto di Saronno
1 oz. Kahlua
½ fill half & half cream
½ fill club soda

WHITE BULL.......................*Build*
Rocks glass, ice
1½ oz. Tequila
½ oz. Kahlua
½ oz. half & half cream

WHITE CADILLAC...............*Build*
Highball glass, ice
1 oz. Scotch
Fill with half & half cream

WHITE HEART.........*Shake or Blend*
Cocktail or house specialty glass, chilled
¾ oz. Sambuca
¾ oz. White Creme de Cacao
2 oz. half & half cream

WHITE LADY
See APPENDICITUS

WHITE MINNESOTA............*Build*
Highball glass, ice
1 oz. White Creme de Menthe
Fill with club soda

WHITE MONKEY
See BANSHEE

WHITE RUSSIAN.................*Build*
Rocks glass, ice
1½ oz. Vodka
½ oz. Kahlua
½ oz. half & half cream

WHITE RUSSIAN, PREMIUM
.....................*Build*
Rocks glass or brandy snifter, ice
1½ oz. Stolichnaya Vodka
½ oz. Tia Maria
½ oz. Bailey's Irish Cream

WHITE SPIDER.....................*Build*
a.k.a. COSSACK
Rocks glass, ice
1½ oz. Vodka
½ oz. White Creme de Menthe

WHITE SWAN.......................*Build*
Rocks glass or brandy snifter, ice
1½ oz. Amaretto di Saronno
½ oz. half & half cream

WHITE WAY..........................*Build*
Rocks glass, ice
1½ oz. Gin
½ oz. White Creme de Menthe

WIKI WAKI WOO
.........*Shake & Strain*
House specialty glass, ice
1 oz. Amaretto di Saronno
½ oz. Vodka
½ oz. Light Rum
½ oz. 151 proof Rum
½ oz. Tequila
1 oz. pineapple juice
1 oz. orange juice
1 oz. cranberry juice
Orange slice and cherry garnish
Orchid garnish optional

WILD ORCHID.........*Shake & Strain*
Bucket glass, ice
1¼ oz. Sambista Cachaça
½ oz. Creme de Noyaux
1½ oz. fresh lime juice
½ oz. grenadine
Orange slice and cherry garnish

WINDEX..................*Shake & Strain*
Rocks glass, chilled
1½ oz. Vodka
¾ oz. Light Rum
½ oz. Blue Curaçao
½ oz. Rose's lime juice

WINE COBBLER.....................*Build*
Wine glass or goblet, ice
4 oz. White wine
1 oz. Triple Sec
½ fill orange juice
½ fill sweet 'n' sour
Splash club soda
Lemon twist garnish

WINE COOLER.....................*Build*
Wine glass or goblet, ice
½ fill requested Wine
½ fill Seven-up
Lemon twist garnish

WOO WOO
See SILK PANTIES

XAVIERA..................*Shake or Blend*
Cocktail or house specialty glass, chilled
½ oz. Kahlua
½ oz. Creme de Noyaux
½ oz. Triple Sec
1½ oz. half & half cream

YALE COCKTAIL.........*Stir & Strain*
Cocktail glass, chilled
1½ oz. Gin
½ oz. Dry Vermouth
2 dashes Angostura bitters
2 dashes simple syrup
Lemon twist garnish

YELLOW BIRD.......................*Build*
Bucket glass, ice
¾ oz. Galliano
¾ oz. Light Rum
½ fill pineapple juice
½ fill orange juice

YELLOW DEVIL....................*Build*
Bucket glass, ice
1 oz. Galliano
1 oz. Mount Gay Eclipse Rum
Fill with orange juice

YELLOW JACKET
See BLACK-EYED SUSAN

YUKON STINGER.................*Build*
Rocks glass, ice
1½ oz. Vodka
¾ oz. Yukon Jack

ZANZIBAR DUNES
.........*Blend with ice*
House specialty glass
1½ oz. Vodka
1 oz. Midori
1 oz. Peach Schnapps
2 oz. orange juice
1½ oz. cranberry juice
½ oz. concord grape juice

ZA-ZA....................*Shake & Strain*
Collins glass, ice
1½ oz. Gin
1½ oz. Dubonnet
½ oz. Triple Sec
2 oz. orange juice

ZIPPER HEAD....................*Build*
Rocks glass, ice
1½ oz. Absolut Vodka
¾ oz. Chambord
Splash club soda

ZOMBIE.................*Shake & Strain*
Collins glass, ice
1½ oz. Myers's Jamaican Rum
½ oz. Creme de Noyaux
½ oz. Triple Sec
1½ oz. sweet 'n' sour
1½ oz. orange juice
Orange slice and cherry garnish

Z STREET SLAMMER
.........*Shake & Strain*
Rocks glass, chilled
1¼ oz. Myers's Jamaican Rum
¾ oz. Creme de Banana
¾ oz. pineapple juice
Dash grenadine

ZUMA BUMA.......................*Build*
Bucket glass, ice
1½ oz. Absolut Citron
½ oz. Chambord
Fill with orange juice
Splash cranberry juice

NON-ALCOHOLIC DRINK RECIPES

A. S. MACPHERSON
.........Shake & Strain
House specialty glass, ice
5 oz. orane juice
3 dashes Angostura bitters
1½ oz. sweet 'n' sour
Shake and strain
Fill with club soda
Orange slice and cherry garnish

BANANA SMASH
.....................Blend with ice
House specialty glass, chilled
1 oz. orgeat
1 ripe banana
2 oz. coconut syrup
3 oz. half & half cream
Whipped cream garnish

CARDINALI............*Shake & Strain*
Bucket glass, ice
3 oz. cranberry juice
2 oz. sweet 'n' sour
Shake and strain
Fill with club soda
Lime wheel garnish

CARDINAL PUNCH
.........Shake & Strain
Bucket glass, ice
1 oz. sweet 'n' sour
1½ oz. orange juice
3 oz. cranberry juice
Shake and strain
Fill with ginger ale

CARTLAND CURE
.........Blend with ice
House specialty glass, chilled
1 whole egg
1 ripe banana
2 tbsp. plain yogurt
1 tbsp. powdered cocoa
1 tsp. honey
1 tsp. wheat germ
3 oz. milk

CINDERELLA............*Shake or Blend*
House specialty glass, chilled
½ oz. grenadine
1½ oz. orange juice
1½ oz. sweet 'n' sour
1½ oz. pineapple juice
Shake and strain or blend with ice
Fill with club soda

GEORGIA'S OWN
.........Blend with ice
House specialty glass, chilled
1½ oz. orange juice
¾ oz. sweet 'n' sour
3 oz. peach nectar
Blend with ice
Fill with club soda

HIMBEERSAFT....................*Build*
Highball glass, ice
3 oz. raspberry syrup
Fill with club soda
Mint sprig garnish

JERSEY LILY...............*Stir & Strain*
Wine glass, chilled
2 dashes non-alcoholic bitters
¼ tsp. sugar
5 oz. carbonated apple juice
Orange slice and cherry garnish

JOGGER.............................*Build*
Bucket glass, ice
½ oz. Rose's lime juice
1 pkg. artificial sweetener optional
Lime wedge garnish

MIAMI VICE............*Shake & Strain*
Bucket glass, ice
½ oz. chocolate syrup
2 oz. half & half cream
Shake and strain
½ fill with root beer
½ fill with cola

MONTEGO BAY
.........*Shake & Strain*
House specialty glass, ice
½ oz. Rose's lime juice
½ oz. grenadine
1 egg yolk
2 oz. sweet 'n' sour
2 oz. orange juice
Shake and strain
Fill with club soda
Lime wedge garnish

NICOLAS...............*Shake & Strain*
House specialty glass, ice
½ oz. grenadine
1 egg white
2 oz. orange juice
2 oz. sweet 'n' sour
2 oz, grapefruit juice
Shake and strain
Fill with club soda

PARSON'S PARTICULAR
.........*Shake & Strain*
White wine glass, chilled
1 egg yolk
½ oz. grenadine
1½ oz. sweet 'n' sour
3 oz. orange juice
Orange slice and cherry garnish

POM POM...............*Shake & Strain*
White wine glass, chilled
1 egg white
½ oz. grenadine
1½ oz. sweet 'n' sour
4½ oz. lemonade
Shake and strain
Fill with club soda
Lemon wedge garnish

PRAIRIE OYSTER..................*Build*
Old Fashion glass, NO ice
1 egg yolk
2 dashes wine vinegar
1 tsp. Worchestershire sauce
1-2 dashes Tabasco sauce
½ tsp. salt
2 oz. tomato juice
Stir gently; do not break egg yolk

PRINCESS MARGARET
.........*Blend with ice*
House specialty glass, chilled
Rim with grenadine and sugar
2-3 dashes raspberry syrup
5-6 large strawberries
1 pineapple slice
1½ oz. sweet 'n' sour
1½ oz. orange juice
Strawberry garnish

ROSY PIPPIN............*Shake & Strain*
White wine glass, ice
½ oz. grenadine
½ oz. sweet 'n' sour
4½ oz. apple juice
Shake and strain
Fill with ginger ale
Apple slice garnish

SAGINAW SNOOZE...............*Build*
Coffee mug, heated
1 tsp. honey
3 oz. cranberry juice
3 oz. apple juice
Heat and serve
Lemon slice and cinnamon stick garnish

SAN FRANCISCO
.........*Shake & Strain*
House specialty glass, ice
½ oz. grenadine
1 egg white
1½ oz. orange juice
1½ oz. pineapple juice
1½ oz. sweet 'n' sour
1½ oz. grapefruit juice
Shake and strain
Fill with club soda
Fresh fruit garnish

SONOMA NOUVEAU............*Build*
White wine glass, ice
5 oz. alcohol-free dry white wine
Fill with club soda
Float ¾ oz. cranberry juice
Lemon twist garnish

SOUTHERN BELLE...............*Build*
Old fashion glass, chilled
2 sprigs fresh mint
½ oz. simple syrup
½ oz. sweet 'n' sour
Muddle contents
Add ice cubes
Fill with ginger ale
Mint sprig garnish

STRAWBERRY ORANGEANA
.........Blend with ice
House specialty glass, chilled
3 oz. orange juice
1 ripe banana
2 oz. strawberry puree
Strawberry and banana garnish

TEMPERANCE COCKTAIL
.........Shake & Strain
Cocktail glass, chilled
½ oz. grenadine
1 egg yolk
3 oz. sweet 'n' sour

WHAT, ME WORRY?*..............Build*
House specialty glass, ice
Salted rim optional
4 oz. alcohol-free beer
Fill with Bloody Mary mix
Lime wedge & peeled shrimp garnish

GLASSWARE

BEER MUG
Capacity: 10 oz. - 16 oz.
Function: Service of draft or bottled beer
Commercial uses: Used also for the service of mixed beer drinks.

BRANDY SNIFTER
a.k.a. BRANDY INHALER
Capacity: 3 oz. - 34 oz.
Function: Service of brandy neat
Commercial uses: Used also as a house specialty glass for mixed drinks served neat, ice cream drinks, frozen drinks and rocks drinks such as Kahlua & cream.

BUCKET GLASS
a.k.a. DOUBLE OLD FASHION, ENGLISH HIGHBALL
Capacity: 12 oz. - 15 oz.
Function: Service of a double portioned mixed drinks.
Commercial uses: Used also to serve tall highballs, tall mixed drinks, and cocktails served on-the-rocks.

CHAMPAGNE SAUCER
Capacity: 3 oz. - 10 oz.
Function: Service of Champagne or sparkling wine.
Commercial uses: Also used to serve straight-up cocktails and Frappés.

CHAMPAGNE TULIP
Capacity: 6 oz. - 9 oz.
Function: Service of Champagne or sparkling wine.
Commercial uses: Also used to serve Champagne-based cocktails.

COCKTAIL GLASS
Capacity: 3 oz. - 5 oz.
Function: Service of straight-up cocktails
Note: Cocktail glasses require chilling prior to service of straight-up cocktails.

COFFEE MUG
Capacity: 9 oz. - 10 oz.
Function: Service of hot drinks
Note: Coffee mugs require preheating to best ensure against cracking due to thermal shock.

COLLINS GLASS
a.k.a. CHIMNEY GLASS
Capacity: 10 oz. - 14 oz.
Function: Service of tall mixed drinks.

CORDIAL GLASS
a.k.a. PONY GLASS
Capacity: 1 oz. - 3 oz.
Function: Service of liqueurs and cordials neat.
Commercial uses: Used also to serve layered cordial drinks.

COUPETTE GLASS
Capacity: 5 oz. - 9 oz.
Function: Service of blended cocktails, cream/ice cream drinks and house specialty drinks.

DOUBLE OLD FASHION GLASS
See BUCKET GLASS

FIESTA GRANDE
a.k.a. MARGARITA
GLASS

Capacity: 12 oz. - 17 oz.
Function: Service of blended or frozen Margaritas, as well as a wide variety of specialty drinks.

FOOTED ALE

Capacity: 10 oz.
Function: Service of draft or bottled beer; most closely associated with service of ale.
Commercial uses: Also used to serve mixed beer drinks.

FOOTED PILSNER

Capacity: 7 oz. - 10 oz.
Function: Service of draft or bottled beer; most closely associated with service of lager.
Commercial uses: Also used to serve mixed beer drinks.

HIGHBALL GLASS

Capacity: 5 oz. - 10 oz.
Function: Service of mixed drinks.

HOUSE SPECIALTY GLASSWARE

A descriptive term used to identify numerous stemmed glassware of various shapes and capacities. House specialty glasses are most frequently used to serve frozen or blended concoctions. Examples include the Coupette, Fiesta Grande, Hurricane, Poco Grande, Squall, Thistle and Zombie.

HURRICANE GLASS

Capacity: 22 oz. - 24 oz.
Function: Service of blended or frozen tropical drinks and house specialty drinks.
Note: The Hurricane is the largest in a series of three specialty glasses that includes the Breeze and Squall.

IRISH COFFEE GLASS

Capacity: 6 oz. - 9 oz.
Function: Service of Irish Coffee and numerous hot drinks.
Note: Irish coffee glasses require preheating to best insure against cracking due to thermal shock.

MIXING GLASS

Capacity: 16 oz.
Function: Used in the preparation of hand-shaken mixed drinks; mixing glass half of a traditional mixing set.
Commercial uses: Also used to serve tall mixed drinks, iced tea and soft drinks.

OLD FASHION GLASS

Capacity: 3 oz. - 10 oz.
Function: Service of Old Fashions, rock drinks and liquors/liqueurs served on-the-rocks.
Note: The heavy, faceted base distinguishes the old fashion glass from a standard rocks glass.

PARFAIT GLASS

Capacity: 4 oz. - 8 oz.
Function: Service of blended or frozen cocktails and tropical drinks, as well as a wide variety of specialty drinks.

POCO GRANDE

Capacity: 10 oz. - 14 oz.
Function: Service of blended or frozen cocktails and tropical drinks, as well as a wide variety of specialty drinks.

PONY GLASS
See CORDIAL GLASS

POUSSE CAFÉ GLASS

Capacity: 2 oz.
Function: Service of Pousse Cafés, numerous other layered cordial drinks and liqueurs served neat.

PRESENTATION SHOT GLASS

Capacity: 1 oz. - 3 oz.
Function: Service of liquor neat
Commercial uses: Also used to serve layered cordial drinks, slammers and chilled shooter drinks.
Note: The heavy, faceted base distinguishes the presentation shot glass from a standard shot glass.

RED WINE BOWL a.k.a. BALLOON GLASS, BOWL

Capacity: 6 oz. - 14 oz.
Function: Service of red wine.
Note: The distinctive bowl shape of the glass facilitates the release of a wine's bouquet.

ROCKS GLASS

Capacity: 5 oz. - 12 oz.
Function: Service of liquor or liqueur on-the-rocks.
Commercial uses: Also used to serve numerous chilled shooter drinks.

SHERRY GLASS

Capacity: 2 oz. - 5 oz.
Function: Service of Sherry, Port, Madeira and Apéritifs neat.
Commercial uses: Also used to serve liqueurs neat and layered cordial drinks.

SHOT GLASS

Capacity: 1 oz. - 2 oz.
Function: Service of liquor neat.
Commercial uses: Also used as a hand-held measuring device.

SNIFTER
See BRANDY SNIFTER

SOUR GLASS

Capacity: 4 oz. - 6 oz.
Function: Service of Sours and Stone Sours straight-up.

SQUALL GLASS

Capacity: 15 oz.
Function: Service of blended or frozen cocktails and tropical drinks, as well as a wide variety of specialty drinks.
Note: The Squall is the second largest in a series of three specialty glasses that includes the Breeze and Hurricane.

THISTLE GLASS

Capacity: 21 oz.
Function: Service of blended or frozen cocktails and tropical drinks, as well as a wide variety of specialty drinks.

WHITE WINE GLASS

Capacity: 10 oz. - 19 oz.
Function: Service of white or blush wines, and wine-based drinks.

Alexis Lichine's New Encyclopedia of Wines &
Spirits. Alexis Lichine. Alfred A. Knopf. New
York. 1985.

American Bartenders School Guide to Drinks. Jack
Tiano. Rutledge Press. New York. 1981

Bar Guide — Here's How! Lawrence Blochman.
New American Library. New York. 1957.

Bartender's Cherry - 2nd edition. Mark Torre.
International Bar Research. 1987.

Bartending...Complete Manual of Professional
Bartending. James Starcevic. American
Bartenders' Association. Sarasota. 1984.

Bartender's Guide. Patrick Duffy. Simon &
Schuster. New York. 1971.

Bennigan's Do-It-Yourself Improvement Book.
Myke Gorecki. S & A Restaurant Corp. Dallas.
1989.

Bon Vivant's Companion or How to Mix Drinks.
Jerry Thomas. Alfred Knopf, Inc. New York.
1928.

Book of Cocktails. Jenny Ridgwell H.P. Books.
Tucson. 1986.

Book of Drinking. John Doxat. Tribune Books.
London, U.K. 1973.

Brandies and Liqueurs of the World. Hurst
Hannum & Robert Blumberg. Doubleday & Co.
New York. 1976.

Burke's Complete Cocktail & Drinking Recipes.
Harman Burke. Books, Inc. 1936.

Cheers! Spirited Guide to Liquors and Liqueurs.
Francesca White. Paddington Press, Ltd.
London, U.K. 1977.

Cocktail Book. Michael Walker. H.P. Books.
Tucson. 1980.

Complete Book of Spirits & Liqueurs. Cyril Ray.
MacMillan Publishing Co. New York. 1977.

Complete World Bartender Guide. Bob Sennett,
Editor. Bantam Books. New York. 1986.

Drinks of Hawaii. Paul Dick. Diamond Head
Publishers. Honolulu. 1972.

Drink Recipes from 100 of the Greatest Bars.
Playboy Clubs International. New York. 1979.

Encyclopedia of Shooters. Bob Johnson.
Contemporary Bar Publications. Miami. 1991.

Esquire's Handbook for Hosts. Grosset & Dunlap.
New York. 1949.

Famous Drinks of New Orleans. Express
Publishing Co. New Orleans. 1989.

Famous Drinks of the Virgin Islands. Dea Murray.
Antilles Printing. St. Thomas. 1968.

Fine Art of Mixing Drinks. David Embury.
Doubleday & Co. New York. 1958.

Gentleman's Companion. Charles Baker, Jr. Crown
Publishers. New York. 1946.

Great Drinks Books. James Starcevic. American
Bartenders' Association. Sarasota. 1986.

Grossman's Guide to Wines, Spirits & Beers.
Harold Grossman. Charles Scribner's Sons. New
York. 1974.

Harvard Student Agencies Bartending Course. Ellen
MacDonald, Editor. St. Martin's Press. New
York. 1984.

Indispensable Drinks Book. John Doxat, Chief
Contributing Editor. Van Nostrand and
Reinhold Co. 1981.

Jerry Thomas's Bartending Guide. Jerry Thomas.
Fitzgerald Publishing Co. 1887.

Jones' Complete Bar Book. Stanley Jones. Barguide
Enterprises. Los Angeles. 1977.

Mocktails: Alcohol-Free Cocktails. American
Bartender's Association. Bradenton, FL. 1986.

New American Bartender's Guide. John Poister.
New American Library. 1989.

Non-alcoholic Pocket Bartender's Guide. Jill Cox.
Simon & Schuster. New York. 1988.

Old Waldorf Bar Days. Albert Stevenson Crockett.
Aventine Press. New York. 1931.

Playboy's Host and Bar Book. Thomas Mario.
Playboy Press. Chicago. 1971.

Pocket Bartenders Guide. Michael Jackson. Simon
& Schuster. New York. 1984.

Pocket Guide to Beer. Michael Jackson. Perigee
Books. New York. 1982.

Pour Man's Friend. John Burton. Apéritifs
Publishing Company. Santa Rosa. 1990.

Pouring for Profit. Costas Katsigris & Mary
Porter. John Wiley & Sons. New York. 1984.

Professional Guide to Bartending - 2nd edition.
Robert Plotkin. P.S.D. Publishing Co. Tucson.
1991.

Spirits & Liqueurs. Rosaland Cooper. H.P. Books.
Tucson. 1982.

Total Bar and Beverage Management. Phillip
Moore. Lebhar-Friedman Books. New York.
1981.

Trader Vic's Bartender's Guide. Trader Vic.
Garden City Books. 1972

What, When and How to Drink. Richard Williams
& David Myers. Dell Books. New York. 1955.

Whiskies of Scotland. Derek Cooper. Cornerstone
Library, Inc. 1978.

LIQUORS, LIQUEURS and SYRUPS GLOSSARY

The notation (®) following many of the products in this glossary signifies that the item is a proprietary liquor or liqueur and that the product name is a registered trademark.

ABSOLUT VODKA ® - Produced since 1879 in Ahus, Sweden, from grains grown domestically, 80 and 100 proof. Absolut also produces PEPPAR, a pepper-infused vodka, and the lemon–infused CITRON vodka. 80 proof

AGUARDIENTE - A distilled spirit popular in Spain and South America. There are two types: AGUARDIENTE UVA, made from grapes, and "AGUARDIENTE de CAÑA", produced from sugar cane or molasses. Both are bottled directly from the still without aging or rectification. In Spanish the name means "burning water". 160 proof

AMARETTO - A reddish-brown aromatic liqueur with a sweet almond flavor. The original and best known, AMARETTO DI SARONNO ® , is made from a 400 year old recipe of neutral spirits, herbs and apricot pits. 54-56 proof

AMER PICON ® - A bitter French cordial made with a base of Spanish oranges, roots, barks, herbs, wine and brandy. Usually mixed with water and consumed as an aperitif. 78 proof

ANGOSTURA BITTERS ® - A dark red, aromatic bitters with a gentian root flavor, made in Trinidad from an infusion of roots, herbs, bark and seeds on a rum base. 45% alcohol by volume

ANISETTE (Anis, Anise) - A sweet, aromatic, licorice-flavored liqueur. The oil of anise in anisette will cause it to turn milky white when mixed with water 50-60 proof

APPLE BRANDY - Produced principally in the United States as APPLE JACK and in France as CALVADOS.

APPLE JACK - An American brandy with a distinctive apple flavor and bouquet, distilled in patent stills from ripe cider apples and aged 2–4 years. 100 proof

APPLETON JAMAICAN RUM ® - Produced by Wray & Nephew since 1749 and sold in several styles: white and gold, 80 proof, Appleton Dark, 80 and 97 proof, and APPLETON RARE aged 12 years, 86 proof. Marketed as the world's oldest rum, APPLETON ESTATE EXTRA is an aromatic, extremely flavorful rum blended and bottled near the Black River Valley. It is aged in new oak casks for a minimum of 12 years, with 27-year-old rum added for character. 86 proof

ATTAKISKA VODKA ® - A dry vodka produced in Anchorage, Alaska made from the pristine waters of 10,000 year old glaciers. 80 proof

AQUAVIT (AKVAVIT) - A spirit produced in the Scandinavian countries from either grain or potatoes, twice-distilled, unaged, usually dry to the taste, and derives its unique flavor principally from caraway seed. 84-90 proof

ARMAGNAC - An aromatic, full-bodied brandy produced in the French province of Gascony. It is produced in continuous stills and aged in black oak casks. There are several styles: Three Star Armagnacs are aged at least 3 years; V.S.O.P. Armagnacs are aged for 4–10 years; Napoleons, Extras, and Hors d' Age are between 15- and 25–years-old. All the versions have a distinctive, robust flavor and bouquet and are drier and lighter-bodied than Cognac. 80-86 proof

BACARDI RUMS ® - Begun in Cuba in 1862, the Bacardi distillery was relocated to Puerto Rico after the Cuban revolution in the early 1960's. The Bacardi name has become synonymous with light-bodied Puerto Rican rums including the best-selling BACARDI LIGHT, the dry and lightly hued BACARDI AMBER, and the full-bodied and rich BACARDI BLACK LABEL, all 80 proof. The top-of-the-line Bacardi rum, BACARDI AÑEJO GOLD RESERVE, is aromatic, smooth, and aged 6 years in wood, 80 proof. Bacardi also makes a 151-proof light rum.

BAILEY'S IRISH CREAM ® - A beige-colored cream liqueur made in Ireland from a compound of coffee, chocolate, Irish whiskey, and fresh dairy cream. The alcohol content allows it to be kept without refrigeration for an extended period of time. 34 proof

BARBADOS RUMS - Distilled from fermented molasses and deriving its distinctive taste from flavorings such as limes, coconut shell, vegetable roots, bitter almonds and raisins, these rums are considered more flavorful than Puerto Rican rums and lighter-bodied than

Jamaican or Martinique rums. Some Barbados rums are flavored with sherry or Madeira. One popular label is Mount Gay. 90-100 proof

BEAM (JIM) BOURBON ® - Established in 1795, the Jim Beam Distilling company of Clermont, Kentucky, produces several straight bourbon whiskies: the best-selling WHITE LABEL SOUR MASH, aged for 52 months, 80 proof; BLACK LABEL, aged for more than 8 years, 90 proof; Bottled-in-Bond, aged 8 years, 100 proof; a straight RYE WHISKEY, 80 proof; and their top-of-the-line BOOKER NOE, a premium straight whiskey bottled in limited quantity and aged 6–8 years, 121.4 proof.

BEEFEATER GIN ® - A popular and extremely dry London dry gin with a pronounced flavor and bouquet, produced since the early 1800's by the family-owned House of Burrough. 94 proof

BENEDICTINE D.O.M. ® - An amber-colored liqueur made from a secret recipe of more than two dozen herbs, plants and peels on a base of Comandon Cognac and aged for 4 years. Originated by the Benedictine Monks at their monastery in Fecamp, France, in 1510, Benedictine D.O.M. is thought to be the oldest liqueur still in production. The initials D.O.M. stand for "Deo Optimo Maximo — "To God, Most Good, Most Great." 80 proof

BENEDICTINE & BRANDY ® - A delicate blend of Benedictine D.O.M. and Comandon V.S.O.P. Cognac (60:40 ratio), produced in Fecamp, France. Benedictine & Brandy is slightly drier than Benedictine D.O.M. due to the addition of V.S.O.P. Cognac. 80 proof

BLACKBERRY BRANDY
See FRUIT BRANDIES

BLACK DEATH VODKA ® - A dry Belgian vodka distilled entirely from sugar beets and made from a recipe dating back to Iceland in 1906. 80 proof

BLUE CURAÇAO - An orange-flavored liqueur, slightly sweeter than Triple Sec, produced from the dried peels of oranges grown on the island of Curaçao. 60 proof (See also CURAÇAO)

BOMBAY GIN ® - An aromatic dry gin, distilled and bottled in London from a recipe dating back to 1761, 86 proof. Bombay also produces SAPPHIRE, an aromatic, extremely dry and flavorful super-premium London Dry gin named after the most celebrated jewel on the Indian subcontinent. 94 proof

BOURBON WHISKEY - A uniquely smooth, full-bodied and full-flavored American straight whiskey. First produced in the late 1700's in Bourbon County, Kentucky, it is distilled principally from fermented corn mash and, to a lesser degree, from rye, wheat, and barley. Under federal regulations, bourbon must be aged a minimum of 2 years in new, charred-oak casks. Most bourbons are aged 4 – 8 years, and bottled between 80 – 86.8 proof. For a whiskey to be identified as a Kentucky bourbon, it must be aged at least one year in the state of Kentucky.

BRANDY - An aged, distilled spirit produced in scores of countries around the world from grapes or a fermented mash of fruit.

BUSHMILLS WHISKEY ® - The Bushmills distillery, in operation since 1608, produces two pot-stilled blended whiskies. WHITE LABEL is a slightly heavy, slightly sweet, 9-year-old Irish whisky. BLACK BUSH, produced in limited quantity, is a single-malt whiskey of superior quality, earning it the reputation as the "Cognac of Ireland." Black Bush is triple-distilled in a copper alembic still, blended and then aged between 9–11 years in oak casks previously used to age sherry. 80 proof

BYRRH ® - An herb- and quinine-flavored, red French fortified aperitif wine; pronounced like "beer".

CACHAÇA - A dry Brazilian rum distilled from sugar cane. 80 proof

C. J. WRAY DRY RUM ® - A clear, estate-bottled, hand-blended rum made in Kingston, Jamaica. 80 proof

CALVADOS APPLE BRANDY - Named after the town of Calvados, in Normandy, France, it is distilled in pot stills from a mash of fermented cider apples. It is aged in oak casks for three to ten years before blending and bottling. V.O. Calvados is aged at least four years, and V.S.O.P. a minimum of five years. Pays d' Auge is the finest Calvados-producing region in Normandy. 80–90 proof

CAMPARI APERITIVO ® - A red bitter Italian aperitif liqueur produced by an infusion of aromatic and bitter herbs, and orange peels. 48 proof

CANADIAN CLUB ® - Produced by Hiram Walker distillers in Ontario, Canada, since the late 1800's, it is a popular, six-year-old blended Canadian Whisky. CANADIAN CLUB CLASSIC is a premium 12-year-old blend. Both are 80 proof.

CANADIAN WHISKY - First distilled in the 1830's by Scottish immigrants (explaining the Scotch spelling of "whisky"), Canadian whisky by law must be blended from cereal grains. It is distilled from a fermented mash of corn, rye and barley. It is often mistakenly identified as a rye whisky; in fact, however, seven times as much corn is used than the other grains. Canadian whiskies are light-bodied, slightly pale and have a reputation for being mellow. Most are aged 6–8 years in oak casks. 80–86.8 proof

CAPTAIN MORGAN'S RUM ® - Produced by Seagrams and made in two styles: BLACK LABEL is distilled from Jamaican, Guyanan, Barbados rums and blended in England, 80 proof; CAPTAIN MORGAN'S SPICED RUM is an aromatic and flavorful blend of aged Puerto Rican rum and various spices, including clove, allspice, and cinnamon. 70 proof

CARPANO PUNT E MES ® - The original blended Vermouth bottled and commercially marketed by Antonio Carpano Turin, Italy, in 1786. The bittersweet aperitif is made from Piedmont wines and Canelli Muscats, and contains not less than 28.8% grape spirits. Carpano also produces a BIANCO (dry) and CLASSICO (sweet) Vermouth.

CHAMBERY - A light French vermouth made in four styles: dry, sweet, the bittersweet AMERICANO, and the wild strawberry flavored CHAMBERYZETTE 17-18% alcohol by volume

CHAMBORD LIQUEUR ROYALE de FRANCE ® - A French framboise liqueur made from small black raspberries and various other fruit, herbs and honey. 33 proof

CHAMBRAISE (CHAMBERYZETTE) - A dry, French vermouth flavored with the juice of wild alpine strawberries.

CHARTREUSE, GREEN ® - A dry and aromatic liqueur produced since 1607 by Carthusian monks at Voiron, France, from a recipe of brandy and 130 wild mountain herbs. This complex compound is redistilled four times before aging. 110 proof

CHARTREUSE, YELLOW ® - A liqueur created by Carthusian monks in 1838, it is sweeter and less aromatic than Green Chartreuse. 80 proof

CHERRY BRANDY
  See FRUIT BRANDIES

CHERRY HEERING (Peter Heering) ® - A tart Danish liqueur produced since 1818, made from the juice and pits of Danish cherries and aged in huge oak vats. It is named after the company's founder, Peter Heering. 49 proof

CHERRY MARNIER ® - French liqueur made with Dalmatian cherries and a brandy base by Lapostolle, the same company that produces Grand Marnier. 48 proof

CHINACO PREMIUM RESERVE ® - A 100% agave tequila, traditionally prepared, aged for 3-4 years in oak, hand-bottled and individually numbered. The silver version is called CALIENTE. 80 proof

CHIVAS REGAL ® - One of the best-selling premium scotches worldwide, established in Aberdeen, Scotland, in 1801; produced in two versions: a 12-year-old blend, 86 proof, and a 21-year-old blend, CHIVAS ROYAL SALUTE, 80 proof. Chivas Regal also produces a honey-flavored, scotch-based liqueur, LOCHAN ORA. 70 proof

CHOCOLAT-SUISSE ® - A chocolate flavored Swiss liqueur marketed with small squares of chocolate in the bottle. 60 proof

COCONUT SYRUP - A non-alcoholic syrup made from the milk and meat of coconuts

COCORIBE ® - A clear, American liqueur made with coconuts and light Virgin Island rum. 60 proof

COGNAC - A brandy made since the early 1600's in the region centered around Jarnac, France, made in pot stills and aged in new Limoges oak casks. To prevent bitterness, the cognac is transferred to previously used casks during the latter stages of aging.

Very old cognacs are removed from their casks and kept in glass containers. This brandy is called "Paradis" and is added to improve other high grades of cognac. A label bearing the name "Grand Champagne" (Large Meadow), or "Petite Champagne" (Small Meadow), means that the cognac was made in that particular region of the Cognac district. "Fine Champagne" indicates a blend of cognac from both regions.

Cognacs are also graded based on their age: "V.S." (Very Special) aged 4–5 years; "V.S.O.P." (Very Superior Old Pale) aged 7–10 years; "V.O." (Very Old) are slightly older and mellower than V.S.O.P.'s; "Napoleon" are usually 15 years old; "X.O." or "X.X.O." (Extra Old) are aged 20–50 years.

COINTREAU ® - An aromatic, classic French Triple Sec produced in Angers, France made from a blend of carefully selected sweet and bitter Mediterranean and tropical orange peels. Cointreau was originally named "Triple Sec White Curaçao", but was renamed when so many other purveyors began marketing similar Triple Sec liqueurs. 80 proof

CORN WHISKEY - Straight corn whiskey is made from a minimum of 80% corn and aged in either new or reused charred-oak barrels for a minimum of 2 years.

COURVOISIER COGNAC ® - Chateau Courvoisier, located in Jarnac, France, owns no vineyard or distillery. It purchases young cognacs from small, local distillers and then ages, blends and markets the brandy under its own label. Courvoisier produces seven grades of cognac: V.S., V.S.O.P., NAPOLEON, X.O., V.O.C.,, a Grande Fine "COUR IMPERIALE" and a blend of extremely old Paradis Cognacs, INITIALE EXTRA. All are 80 proof.

CREME de ALMOND
See CREME de NOYAUX

CREME de BANANA - A banana-flavored cordial. 60 proof.

CREME de CACAO - A liqueur flavored by cacao and vanilla beans, produced in both a clear and dark brown version, with little or no difference between the two other than color. 50-60 proof

CREME de CASSIS - A liqueur flavored by black currants grown principally in the Burgundy region of France. 36-50 proof

CREME de GRAND MARNIER ® - A fresh cream liqueur made with Grand Marnier. 34 proof

CREME de MENTHE - A cordial flavored by various varieties of mint leaves, principally peppermint. Produced in green and clear versions, with the only difference being color. 60 proof

CREME de NOYAUX - A dark red liqueur made from crushed apricot and peach pits with an almond-like flavor. 54–56 proof

CREME de VIOLETTE (CREME de YVETTE) - A liqueur with the rich color and flavor obtained from violet petal oil of essence and vanilla. 60 proof

CROWN ROYAL ® - A super-premium Canadian whisky that was first introduced in 1939 by Seagrams of Canada to celebrate the unprecedented visit of King George VI and Queen Elizabeth. 80 proof

CRYSTAL COMFORT ® - A clear, dry, light-bodied liqueur made by Southern Comfort. 72 proof

CUERENTA y TRES (LICOR 43) ® - A Spanish liqueur made from vanilla, citrus, milk, and forty-three different herbs. 68 proof

CUERVO (JOSE) TEQUILA ® - Founded in 1795 under a grant from the King of Spain, Jose Cuervo produces three widely distributed tequilas: silver, ESPECIAL (gold), and the premium 1800. All are 80 proof.

CURAÇAO - A liqueur flavored primarily by the dried peels of green oranges grown on the island of Curaçao in the Dutch West Indies. It is slightly sweeter in taste than Triple Sec and is produced in clear, orange, red and blue versions.

DANIEL'S (JACK) TENNESSEE WHISKEY ® - A straight Tennessee sour mash whiskey produced since the Civil War in Lynchburg, Tennessee. Jack Daniels "Old Number 7" is distilled from corn, malted barley, rye, and fresh spring water from underground limestone caves. The whiskey is slow filtered through finely ground sugar maple charcoal in 12-foot-high vats. The GREEN LABEL is aged for at least 4 years. The BLACK LABEL is aged for at least 5 years. Both are aged in charcoal-lined oak casks. 86 proof

DEMERARA RUM - Distilled from sugar cane grown along the Demerara River in Guyana, South America. Produced in a column still, it is darker, less aromatic, and slightly less flavorful than Jamaican rum, and marketed at 86, 96, 114, and 151 proof.

DEMI-TASSE CREAM LIQUEUR ® - A fresh cream liqueur flavored with coffee and brandy. 34 proof

DOCTOR McGILLICUDDY'S MENTHOLMINT ® - A dry, menthol-flavored schnapps from Canada. 60 proof

DRAMBUIE ® - A liqueur made from 15-year-old Highland single malt scotch whisky, heather honey, spice and herbs. The name "Drambuie" comes from the Celtic "an dram buidheach," meaning "the drink that satisfies." 80 proof

DRY VERMOUTH - Most closely associated with France, dry vermouth is also produced in Italy, the U.S., and South America. dry vermouth is made from light and thin Picpoul and Clairette wines. These wines are aged for 2-3 years, in oak casks exposed to the elements to accelerate maturation. After blending, the "basic" wine is then infused with special flavoring agents. Each vermouth obtains its unique taste and character from the 30-50 herbs, seeds, roots, plants, and spices used in the infusion process. Alcohol is added to raise the vermouth to 19% alcohol by volume.

DUBONNET ® - A French, quinine-flavored, fortified aperitif wine produced in both BLONDE (dry) and ROUGE (sweet) versions, and marketed at 19% alcohol by volume.

EAU de VIE - A coarse, dry, unaged brandy distilled from fruit and pomace (wine-making remnants). The French name means "water of life."

EL TESORO de DON FELIPE ® - A handmade, estate grown and bottled, 100% agave tequila produced in both the PLATA (silver) and MUY AÑEJO (gold) at the La Alteña distillery located in the Los Altos region of Jalisco, Mexico. It is crafted using traditional techniques more along the lines of a fine Cognac or Bordeaux claret. It is twice distilled in a Cognac-type (alembic) still to exactly 80 proof, a process that leaves the tequila undiluted. The Plata is bottled fresh and unfiltered within 24 hours of distillation. The Muy Añejo is aged in oak barrels for 1-2 years in a stone-walled, humidity controlled cellar.

FALERNUM - A clear liqueur flavored with lime, almond, ginger, spices and sugar. Invented in Barbados, British West Indies, over 200 years ago. 12-18 proof.

FERNET - A type of aromatic Italian bitters. The most popular is "Fernet Branca." 80 proof (see below)

FERNET BRANCA ® - A famous Italian medicinal bitters. FERNET BRANCA MENTA is flavored with fresh mint leaves. 80 proof

FRAISE - A dry French eau de vie made from strawberries.

FRAMBOISE - A dry French eau de vie made from raspberries.

FRANGELICO ® - An Italian liqueur made from a 300-year-old recipe of wild hazelnuts, berries, and spices. 56 proof

FREEZOMINT ® - A semi-sweet French mint liqueur produced by Cusenier.

FRENCH VERMOUTH see DRY VERMOUTH

FRUIT BRANDIES - Made by distilling a fermented mash of fruit, most are bottled at 70 proof although some exceed 100 proof (such as Slivovitz, an Eastern European plum brandy). Popular examples of fruit brandies include apple, blackberry, cherry, peach, plum, raspberry and strawberry.

GALLIANO (Liquore Galliano) ® - A golden, aromatic Italian liqueur made from herbs, spices and seeds, with a pronounced flavor of anise, 70 proof. Named after Major Guiseppe Galliano, a military hero of the late 19th century. The firm Galliano also produces SAMBUCA di GALLIANO and AMARETTO di GALLIANO.

GENEVA (GENEVER) GIN - A blend of malted barley, corn, and rye distilled in a pot still and then redistilled with botanicals such as juniper berries, caraway, and other aromatics. It is full-flavored with a malty taste and bouquet, and has been produced since the late 1600's. It is also called Schiedam, Holland or Dutch gin. There are two styles: OUDE GENEVER, a pungent, full-bodied spirit, and JONGE GENEVER, lighter and more popular. Both styles are aged in wood before bottling. 80 proof

GEORGIA MOONSHINE WHISKEY ® - An unaged corn whiskey marketed in a mason jar. 80 proof

GIN - "London Dry" gin is the best known type of gin. The term "London Dry" refers to style and no longer is a geographical reference. This type of gin is first distilled in a column still, typically from a fermented mash of up to 75% corn, 15% barley malt, and other grains. Purified water is added to reduce the distillate to 120 proof. The reduced spirit is redistilled with flavoring agents called "botanicals," a mixture of roots, herbs, fruits and seeds. Among those frequently used are: Juniper berries, caraway, anise and coriander seeds, lemon and orange peels, and angelica and orris roots. These botanicals give gin its unique flavor and bouquet. The final distillate is again reduced in alcohol content to 80-94 proof, and then bottled. London dry gin is not aged, although it is often stored in glass-lined, stainless steel holding vats prior to bottling. Other, less well known types of gin are GENEVA (Genever) and PLYMOUTH.

GINGER BEER - A carbonated, non-alcoholic, ginger-flavored beverage.

GLENFIDDICH SCOTCH WHISKY ® - A 12 year old, single malt scotch whisky, produced since 1887, with a slightly sweet, smokey flavor. Glenfiddich also produces a 30-year-old single malt scotch. The name Glenfiddich means "Valley of the Deer." 86 proof

(THE) GLENLIVET ® - A 12-year-old Highland single malt scotch whisky with a slight fruity and smoky flavor, produced since 1825 in Scotland's first registered legal distillery. 86 proof

GOLDWASSER (EAU d'OR, LIQUEUR d'OR) - A complex Eastern European liqueur made from a blend of coriander, orange peels, and various other spices and herbs. Produced since the 16th century, when gold was thought to have medicinal properties, it features 22-karat flecks of gold floating in the bottle (hence the name, Goldwasser). 60-80 proof

GRAND MARNIER ® - A French liqueur produced by the Lapostolle family since 1827. Its flavor and bouquet is derived from a delicate blend of wild bitter oranges and fine cognac. There are two styles of Grand Marnier: the more expensive version, CORDON ROUGE, is made with a cognac base and aged for 18 months; the second style, CORDON

JAUNE, is paler in color and made with a lesser-quality brandy, and is not sold in the United States. 80 proof.

GRAND MARNIER CUVEE de CENTENAIRE ® - A version of Grand Marnier (see above) produced to commemorate the 100th anniversary of the liqueur. Drier than the Cordon Rouge Grand Marnier, with a more pronounced cognac flavor and bouquet, 80 proof. Grand Marnier also produces GRAND MARNIER CENTCINQUINTENAIRE, issued to commemorate their 150th anniversary and marketed in a colorful enamel-painted floral bottle. 80 proof

GRAPPA - A sharp, colorless, unaged Italian brandy distilled from grape pomace, the remnants of the wine-making process. Technically an EAU de VIE de MARC.

GRENADINE - A sweet, red, non-alcoholic syrup flavored with pomegranates. In some rare instances grenadine is produced with a low alcohol content.

HAITIAN RUMS - Aromatic and medium-bodied rum made from the unfermented sap of local sugar cane. Often referred to as "brandy rum," Haitian rums are double-distilled in pot stills in the same manner as cognacs, and then aged in wood for 4 to 7 years. Most Haitian rums are exported to and marketed in France. 80-90 proof

HERREDURA TEQUILA ® - Made entirely from the fermented sap of the rare blue agave plant, distilled in pot stills and produced in limited quantity in three styles: a light-bodied silver, a medium-bodied gold, and the aged HERRADURA AÑEJO. 92 proof

IRISH MIST ® - A spicy Irish liqueur made from Irish whiskey, heather honey, clover, and a variety of herbs. 80 proof

IRISH WHISKEY - Considered the oldest of the whiskeys, it is made from a fermented mash of malted and unmalted barley, corn, rye, and lesser amounts of other cereal grains. All Irish whiskeys are triple-distilled in pot stills, and are aged 3 to 9 years in reused sherry, brandy, bourbon or rum oak casks. Irish whiskeys are full-bodied and possess a smooth, malty flavor. 80–90 proof

ITALIAN VERMOUTH
See SWEET VERMOUTH

JACK DANIEL'S TENNESSEE WHISKEY
See DANIEL'S (JACK) TENNESSEE WHISKEY

JÄGERMEISTER ® - A German liqueur made from gentian, and 56 herbs, roots, and fruits. It is purported to have digestive properties. 70 proof

JAMAICAN RUMS - A dark, full-bodied, pungent rum made from sugar cane molasses that is allowed to ferment for up to 3 weeks in large fermentation vats. Residue from previous distillations, called "dunder," is added to hasten the natural fermentation process. This fermented mixture is distilled in traditional pot stills. The distillate produced in the middle of the process is then redistilled. Jamaican Rum is aged in oak puncheon (70-gallon) casks for typically 5 to 7 years, although some are aged for 30 years. Caramel is added to enhance the rum's color. Most Jamaican rums are bottled at 80 to 97 proof, and occasionally at 151 proof.

JAMESON IRISH WHISKEY ® - An Irish whiskey first produced in 1780 in Dublin, Ireland. John Jameson and Son produces four versions of whiskey: the best known is Jameson's White Label, an aromatic, blended whiskey made in a pot still and aged in American charred oak casks, 80 proof; JAMESON CRESTED TEN, a blend of older Irish whiskies and aged in reused sherry casks; 1780, a 12-year-old blend; and JOHN JAMESON VERY SPECIAL OLD WHISKEY.

JUMBY BAY PROPRIETOR'S RUM ® - A light, gold rum made in the West Indies from a blend of premium Antiguan (51%) and Barbados (49%) rums. 86 proof

KAHLUA ® - Mexican liqueur made with coffee beans and cane spirit, 53 proof. Kahlua also produces a bottled cocktail, BLACK RUSSIAN, a blend of vodka and Kahlua, 70 proof

KIRSCH (KIRSCHWASSER) - An aromatic and colorless brandy distilled in a pot still from a fermented mash of black cherries, with a bitter-almond taste. Most frequently produced in France, Switzerland and Germany. 80-90 proof

KÜMMEL - A dry, aromatic European liqueur made with neutral spirits, caraway, cumin, and anise seeds. Some Kümmels have crystallized sugar on the bottom of the bottle and are identified as KÜMMEL CRYSTALLIZE or EISKÜMMEL. 54–86 proof

Le GRANDE PASSION ® - A French liqueur made from passion fruit and Armagnac, produced by the makers of Grand Marnier. 48 proof

LAIRD'S APPLEJACK BRANDY ® - An apple brandy distilled from fermented cider apples in a patent still and aged in oak barrels for 5 years, 80 proof. Laird's also produces LAIRD'S CAPTAIN, aged for 7 1/2 years. 100 proof

LAMB'S NAVY RUM ® - A rich, full-bodied naval rum. It is a mix of rums from Barbados, Guyana, Jamaica, and Trinidad, blended on the Caribbean island of Tortola. 80 proof

LICOR 43
See CUARANTA y TRES

LILLET ® - A semi-dry, fortified aperitif wine with the subtle flavor of oranges, herbs, and quinine, produced in France since 1872 in two versions: a BLONDE (drier and made with white wine) and a ROUGE (sweeter and made with red wine). 18% alcohol by volume

LIQUORE GALLIANO
See GALLIANO

LIQUORE STREGA ® - A spicy Italian liqueur made from a blend of 70 herbs and citrus, originally marketed with a twig in the bottle. The liqueur takes its name from the Italian word for "witch"; it is purported to have been formulated by a coven of witches who used it as a love potion. 80 proof

MAKER'S MARK KENTUCKY BOURON ® - A straight Kentucky bourbon made since 1889 in Lorettor, Kentucky, and marketed in three versions: WHITE LABEL, 90 proof; a limited edition 101 proof; and V.I.P., 90 proof

MALIBU ® - Canadian liqueur made from Jamaican light rum and coconut. 56 proof

MANDARINE NAPOLEON ® - A dry, Belgium liqueur with the flavor and delicate bouquet of Andalusian tangerines and aged Cognac. The GRANDE RESERVE version is prepared with V.S.O.P. cognac. 80 proof

MARASCHINO - A clear, aromatic liqueur made from Dalmatian Marasca cherries and almonds. 50-60 proof

MARTINIQUE RHUM - Flavorful and full-bodied rums made in both light and dark styles from unfermented sugar cane sap distilled and then shipped to Bordeaux, France, for aging in wood. Unaged Martinique rhum, bottled directly from the still, is called GRAPPE BLANCHE RHUM. 80–95 proof

MESCAL (MEZCAL) - A spirit distilled from the fermented juice, roots, and pulp of the Mexican Agave plant, grown in the southwestern states of Mexico. Mescal is a clear, oily brandy and has a distinctive weedy and herbaceous taste. It is unaged and marketed at 80-90 proof. Tradi-tionally bottled with a blue agave root worm.

METAXA BRANDY ® - A sweet, flavorful brandy produced in Greece and marketed in three versions: FIVE-STAR, 82 proof; SEVEN-STAR, 92 proof; and GRANDE FINE, 80 proof.

MIDORI MELON LIQUEUR ® - A Japanese honeydew liqueur produced by Suntory. 46 proof

MOHOLA ® - A Japanese mango-flavored liqueur made from peaches, citrus and apricots. 44 proof

MOUNT GAY ECLIPSE RUM ® - An amber, semi-light sugar cane rum aged for 3 years and produced in Bridgetown, Barbados, 90 proof. Mount Gay also produces the aromatic, flavorful sugar cane rum, RESERVE WHITE. 80 proof .

MYERS'S JAMAICAN RUM ® - Produced in Kingstown, Jamaica since 1879, Myers's is best known for their flavorful and full-bodied Original Dark Rum. It is labeled as the "Planter's Punch Brand", because distiller Fred Myers is credited with creating the now famous drink. Myers's also distills a lighter-bodied GOLDEN RICH JAMAICAN RUM and a dry, light PLATINUM (clear) JAMAICAN RUM. 80 proof

MYERS'S ORIGINAL RUM CREAM ® - A Canadian liqueur made with Myers's Jamaican Rum and fresh cream. 34 proof

NASSAU ROYALE ® - An aromatic liqueur made with 22 herbs and spices, vanilla, and light rum, produced in Nassau, Bahamas. 67 proof

NAVAL RUM - Naval rums are blended from spirits distilled in Barbados, Guyana, Jamaica, and Trinidad. These various rums are shipped and blended on the Island of Tortola in the British Virgin Islands. Since 1660, naval rum has been a standard issue to sailors in the British Royal Navy.

NEW ENGLAND RUMS - Made in colonial America since prior to the American Revolution, New England rums are dark, full-bodied, aromatic, pot-stilled spirits. They are historically famous for their role in the notorious "Triangular trade". This cycle of commerce sent New England rum to Africa in exchange for native Africans, who in turn were sold or traded in the West Indies for raw molasses, which was then shipped to New England for distillation into rum.

OPAL NERA ® - A super premium Sambuca with the hue of black opal, produced in Theme, Italy, and made from anise, elder flower and lemon. 80 proof

ORANGE BITTERS - A bittersweet orange-flavored bitters.

ORANGE FLOWER WATER - A French non-alcoholic perfumed water with the scent of orange blossoms.

ORGEAT - A sweet French non-alcoholic almond-flavored syrup.

OUZO (DOUZICO) - A semi-sweet liqueur made in Greece and Cyprus from anise, slightly sweeter than MASTIC and much drier and stronger than ANISETTE. 90-92 proof

PARFAIT AMOUR - A violet-hued European liqueur, aromatic and sweet, made from a blend of citrus oils, essence of violets, citron, coriander and brandy. 60 proof

PASSION FRUIT SYRUP - A non-alcoholic syrup made from passion fruit juice, sugar and citric acid. Also called "PASSIONOLA."

PEACH BRANDY
  See FRUIT BRANDY

POIRE (PEAR) WILLIAM - An aromatic and quite dry eau de vie, or white brandy, made in Germany, Switzerland and France from the fermented mash of William, Bartlett or Anjou pears. Some versions are aged for 1–2 years and some are marketed with a whole pear in the bottle. 80-90 proof

PEPPERMINT SCHNAPPS - A clear, spicy mint liqueur made from peppermint oils. Lighter and less sweet than CREME de MENTHE. (see also: Schnapps) 60-100 proof

PERNOD ® - An aromatic, pale-yellow ABSINTHE substitute made in France from anise seeds, herbs, flavorings, and a base of brandy. In 1797, Henri-Louis Pernod acquired the recipe for Absinthe, from which this liqueur is derived. Pernod is an elixir similar to Absinthe without the latter's high alcoholic content and the dangerous ingredient "wormwood". 80.2 proof

PETER HEERING
 See CHERRY HEERING.

PEYCHAUD BITTERS ® - An aromatic New Orleans bitters with a pronounced anise flavor. 35% alcohol by volume

PIMM'S CUP NO. 1 ® - A full-bodied, amber liqueur made in England from herbs, spices and lemons on a gin spirit base. Its century-old recipe is named for Pimm's Oyster Bar and Restaurant in the Financial District in London. It was at this restaurant that the original "Gin Sling" was created and later bottled as "Pimm's Cup No. 1", 67 proof. Pimm's produces several other bottled cocktails: PIMM'S NO. 2 has a scotch base; NO. 3 a brandy base; NO. 4 a rum base; NO. 5 a rye whiskey base; and NO. 6 a vodka base.

PISCO BRANDY ®- A fiery, clear pomace brandy made from Muscat wine remnants and aged briefly in clay jars. It is named after a port in southern Peru. 81.6 proof

PLYMOUTH GIN - A full-bodied, aromatic and flavorful spirit distilled since 1793 in a converted monastery and a favorite with sailors of the British Royal Navy based nearby at the port of Plymouth, who popularly add a dash of Angostura bitters to create "Pink Gin".

PUERTO RICAN RUMS - Puerto Rican Rums are distilled in column stills from a fermented mash of sugar cane molasses. Following distillation, the rum is aged in new oak casks from 1 to 4 years and then filtered through charcoal. The gold version is amber-hued and has a fuller flavor than the silver (clear) version. Marketed from 80 to 151 proof.

PUSSER'S BRITISH NAVY RUM ® - A full-bodied rum made from various Caribbean rums blended on the Island of Tortola in the British West Indies. Pusser's Rum has been standard issue to sailors of the British Royal Navy since 1655; its name is a derivation of the word "Purser's". 95.5 proof

RHUM BARBANCOURT ® - A dark, aromatic, medium-bodied rum made on the Island of Haiti from double-distilled unfermented sugar cane sap, and marketed in three ages: 3-year-old, 8-year-old, and 15-year-old. 86 proof

ROSE'S LIME JUICE ® - A reconstituted non-alcoholic sweetened lime juice made since the late 18th century from West India limes in St. Albans, England.

ROYALE MONTAINE ® - A French liqueur made with brandy and oranges. 80 proof

RUM - A distilled spirit produced from a fermented (or occasionally unfermented) mash of sugar cane or sugar cane molasses. Rums are distilled in virtually every country that grows and exports sugar. (see also: Jamaican Rum, Martinique Rhum, Naval Rum, New England Rum, Puerto Rican Rum, and West Indies Rum)

RUMPLE MINZE SCHNAPPS ® - A peppermint schnapps made in the Black Forest of Germany. 100 proof

RYE WHISKEY - An American straight whiskey made from a fermented mash containing a minimum of 51% rye grain, and aged in new charred oak casks for at least 2 years. 80–100 proof

SAKE - A Japanese beer brewed from rice and usually served warm. 14-18% alcohol by volume.

SAMBISTA CACHAÇA ® - A dry Brazilian aguardiente made from cane sugar. 80 proof

SAMBUCA - An Italian anise-flavored liqueur made from wild Elderbush Berries. Traditionally, Sambuca is sipped "neat" with three coffee beans. 70-84 proof

SAUZA TEQUILA ® - Tequilas produced by Sauza since 1878 and marketed in four versions: an unaged silver and gold, the 100% agave HORNITOS, CONMEMORATIVO AÑEJO, and TRES GENERACIONES. 80 proof

SCHNAPPS - A semi-dry liqueur produced primarily in Europe and flavored by any one of a multitude of flavors, such as apple, banana, blueberry, butterscotch, chocolate, cinnamon, coffee, licorice, orange, peach, peppermint, root beer, spearmint, wilderberry (berry) and wintergreen.

SCOTCH WHISKY - Whisky has been made in Scotland since the late 1500's. It is distilled primarily from barley which is allowed to germinate, or malt. The grain is dried in a kiln over a peat fire, permeating the barley malt with the aroma and flavor of peat smoke, which will later be imparted to the whisky. There are essentially three types of Scotch whisky: malt, grain, and blended.

Malt Scotch Whisky - generally full-bodied, full-flavored, 10- to 12-years-old, with a distinctive, smokey, peaty taste. The majority are called "single malts", meaning they are straight, unblended whiskies from a single distillery. Most single malts come from the Highlands of Scotland, although fine malt Scotch is also produced on the islands of Islay, Skye, and in Campbelton in the Lowlands.

Grain Scotch Whisky - A light-bodied whisky distilled in a continuous still from cereal grains and produced almost entirely in the Lowlands of Scotland. While occasionally marketed straight, this whisky is most frequently used in the blending of other Scotch whiskies.

Blended Scotch Whisky - The majority of scotches are combinations of grain and malt whiskies blended to a unique and closely guarded recipe. The difference between various blended Scotches comes from both proportion and quality of the component whiskies.

SEAGRAM'S SEVEN CROWN ® - A flavorful blended whiskey made in Lawrenceburg, Indiana, since the 1930's. It has been America's best-selling whiskey since the 1950's. 80 proof

SEAGRAM'S V.O. CANADIAN ® - A 6-year-old blended Canadian whisky. 80 proof

SLOE GIN - An aromatic prunelle liqueur with a flavor reminiscent of cherry. It is made from the Sloe Berry, a small wild plum that grows on the Blackthorn bush. One style of Sloe Gin is marketed as "Creamy Top" and produces a froth when shaken or blended. 40-60 proof

SMIRNOFF VODKA ® - An American, charcoal-filtered vodka made from corn by Heublein in Connecticut since the 1930's. Long the best-selling vodka in America, and produced in four versions: WHITE LABEL, 80 proof, SMIRNOFF de

CZAR, 82.6 proof, SMIRNOFF SILVER, 90.4 proof,, and SMIRNOFF BLUE LABEL, 100 proof.

Piotr Smirnoff established the Smirnoff distillery in Moscow in 1818. Shortly thereafter, Czar Alexander III made Smirnoff the sole purveyor of vodka to the Imperial Russian Court. By the beginning of World War I, Smirnoff was producing one million bottles a day. The Russian Revolution forced Smirnoff and his family to flee Russia, eventually settling in Paris. The famous formula for Smirnoff Vodka made its way to Connecticut and the Heublein firm in 1934.

SOUTHERN COMFORT ® - An American liqueur produced since 1875 from a blend of bourbon whiskey, peach liqueur, and freshly peeled and pitted peaches. It is aged and mellowed in oak barrels for at least 8 months. 80 and 100 proof (also see CRYSTAL COMFORT)

STOLICHNAYA VODKA ® - Pure grain vodkas produced in Russia's oldest distillery. In addition to their standard 80- and 100-proof versions, Stolichnaya makes PERTSOVKA, a dark brown pepper-flavored vodka made from cayenne, capsicum and cubeb peppers, 70 proof, OKHOTNICHYA, an herb- and honey-flavored vodka, 90 proof, LIMONNAYA, a lemon-flavored vodka, 80 proof, and CRISTALL, an ultra-premium, distilled in limited quantity from winter wheat and filtered glacial water, 80 proof.

STREGA
  See LIQUORE STREGA

STUBBS QUEENSLAND RUM ® - A superpremium dry white rum distilled from sugar cane in Queensland, Australia. 80 proof

SWEET VERMOUTH - Most closely associated with Italy, sweet vermouth is now also produced in France, the U.S., Spain and various other countries. Most Italian vermouths are produced from Apulia and Moscato di Canelli wines. These wines are infused with secret formulas of flavoring agents consisting of herbs, roots, seeds, quinine, and various botanicals. The vermouth is then aged 1–2 years, blended, filtered, and fortified with distilled spirits. Sweet vermouth contains 16–18% alcohol by volume.

TANQUERAY GIN ® - A full-bodied London dry gin distilled at Finsbury, England, at one time a health spa known for the purity of its water. 94.6 proof

TENNESSEE WHISKEY - A whiskey distilled in Tennessee from a fermented mash of grain, primarily corn. The whiskey is then filtered through finely-ground sugar maple charcoal and aged in charred oak barrels for a minimum of 4 years. 90 proof

TEQUILA - A spirit produced in or near the town of Tequila in Jalisco, Mexico, from the fermented, sweet sap of the Agave Tequilana Weber, known in Mexico as the Mezcal plant and in the U.S. as the Century plant. The sap is extracted from the plant's pulpy heart, allowed to ferment, and then double-distilled in copper pot stills. Tequila is marketed in three styles: the unaged silver, often bottled immediately following distillation; gold, aged in oak vats for 1–2 years; and Añejo, "the aged one", between 1 and 3 years old. 80–92 proof

TIA MARIA ® - A liqueur produced from a blend of Blue Mountain coffee beans, chocolate, and Jamaican rum, made in Jamaica since the late 1700's. It is lighter and drier than Kahlua and considered the original coffee liqueur. 53 proof

TUACA ® - A complex, semi-sweet Italian liqueur made with herbs, fruit peels and brandy, from a 500-year-old recipe. 84 proof

VANDERMINT ® - A rich Dutch chocolate and mint liqueur, made in Southern Holland since the 1500's. 60 proof

VODKA - A spirit distilled from a fermented mash of potatoes, rice, beets, grapes, and (most frequently) grain. The fermented mash is distilled in a continuous still to a high-proof alcohol, then filtered and reduced to 80-100 proof. The majority of vodkas are unaged and bottled immediately after distillation. Western vodkas are neutral in taste, odorless and colorless, while Russian and Eastern European vodkas retain taste, color, or are flavored with various items.

WEST INDIES RUM - The general classification for rums produced in Trinidad, Barbados, Jamaica, and Guyana.

WILD TURKEY BOURBON ® - A straight bourbon whiskey produced in Lawrenceberg, Kentucky, since 1855 in three styles, BLACK LABEL, 80 proof; 12-year-old WHITE LABEL, 101 proof; and single-cask, barrel-proof RARE BREED, 109.6 to 110 proof. Wild Turkey also makes a straight RYE WHISKEY, 101 proof.

YUKON JACK ® - A semi-sweet Canadian liqueur made with herbs, orange peels and Canadian whisky, 100 proof. Yukon Jack also produces GOLD RESERVE, a drier, darker version of the original liqueur made with premium 6-year-old Canadian whisky, 86 proof.

INDEX
Drink Recipes
by Ingredient and Drink Type

111

Dry Rob Roy (Scotch)	68
Latin Manhattan (light rum)	48
Manhattan (bourbon)	48
New Orleans Manhattan (bourbon)	48
Perfect Brandy Manhattan	48
Perfect Manhattan (bourbon)	48
Perfect Rob Roy (Scotch)	68
Perfect Comfort Manhattan	48
Paddy (Irish)	60
Rob Roy (Scotch)	68
Southern Comfort Manhattan	48

MARGARITAS

Apple Margarita	49
Black Gold Margarita	49
Blue Margarita	49
Blue Moon Margarita	49
Britannia Margarita	49
Cactus Rose Margarita	49
Cadillac Margarita	49
Cajun Margarita	49
Catalina Margarita	49
Chinacout Margarita	49
Fruit Margarita	50
Georgia Margarita	50
Gold Margarita	50
Green Iguana	50
Italian Margarita	50
Jamaican Margarita	50
Kentucky Margarita	50
Key Lime Margarita	50
Mad Russian Margarita	50
Maximilian Margarita	50
Mango Margarita	50
Margarita	48
Margarita Amore	48
Maui Margarita	50
Melon Margarita	50
Midnight Margarita	49
Midnight Madness Margarita	51
Mount Fugi Margarita	51
Orange Margarita	51
Pear Margarita	51
Pineapple Margarita	51
Purple Gecko	51
Purple Margarita	51
Raspberry Margarita	51
Red Hot Margarita	51
Rolls Royce Margarita	51
Rosarita Margarita	51
Sonoran Margarita	51
Tuaca Margarita	52
Vintner's Margarita	52
Virgin Margarita	52

MARTINIS & GIBSONS

Black Martini	52
Boston Martini	52
Buckeye Martini	52
Cajun King Martini	52
Cajun Martini	52
Dry Gibson	31
Dry Martini	52
Dry Vodka Gibson	32
Dry Vodka Martini	52
Dutch Martini	52
Extra Dry Gibson	31
Extra Dry Martini	52
Extra Dry Vodka Martini	53
Fidel's Martini	53
French Martini	53
Gibson	31
Hot Martini	53

Martini	52
Nutcracker Martini	53
Paisley	53
Perfect Cocktail	53
Perfect Martini	53
Riviera Martini	53
Sake Martini	53
Spanish Martini	53
Strawberry Martini	53
Vodka Gibson	32
Vodka Martini	53

MIDORI MELON LIQUEUR

Artificial Intelligence	6
Balashi Breeze	7
Bahama Piña Colada	62
Bullfrog (2)	13
Cactus Piña Colada	63
Cheap Shades	20
Citron Neon	21
Cold Fusion	22
Colorado River Cooler	22
Crystal Clear	23
Done & Bradstreet	26
Electric Watermelon	27
E. T.	27
Gang Green	31
Green Eyes	33
Green Iguana	50
Green Russian	34
Green Sneakers	34
Gumby	34
Honeydew	36
Jamaican Crawler	40
Killer Koolaid	43
Kool Aid	44
Kuwaiti Cooler	44
Leaf	45
Malibu Fizz	47
Mediterranean Freeze	53
Mellonaire	54
Melon Ball	54
Melon Ball Cooler	54
Melon Breeze	54
Melon Grind	54
Melon Kamikaze	42
Melon Margarita	50
Melon Moose	54
Melon Scoop	54
Midorable	55
Midori Driver	55
Midori Piña Colada	63
Midori Stinger	56
Pacific Rim	60
Pearl Harbor	61
Sex on the Beach (2) (5)	73
Spats Columbo	76
Straight Shooter	77
Torque Wrench	82
Traffic Light (2)	82
Tropical Hooter	83
Tropical Hut	83
Tuaca Pousse Café	65
Wall Street Wizard	84
Watermelon (2) (4)	85
What Crisis?	85
Zanzibar Dunes	87

MOUNT GAY ECLIPSE RUM

Bananas Barbados	7
Caribbean Grid Lock	19
Jamaican Barbados Bomber	40
Jamba Juice	41

Index of Drink Recipes

125

Iced Tea, Hawaiian	37
Iced Tea, Long Beach	37
Iced Tea, Long Island	38
Iced Tea, Raspberry	38
Italian Margarita	50
Key Lime Margarita	50
Lighthouse	46
Loco En La Cabeza	46
Mango Margarita	50
Margarita	48
Maui Margarita	50
Melon Margarita	50
Mexican Coffee	55
Mexican Runner	55
Orange Margarita	51
Panther	60
Pear Margarita	51
Pineapple Margarita	51
Prairie Fire	65
Purple Gecko	51
Purple Margarita	51
River Madness	68
Rodeo Driver	69
Salty Bull	70
Sicilian Sunrise	73
Silver Bullet	74
Spanish Fly (2)	76
Spike	76
Stockmarket Zoo	77
Sunburn	78
Tarnished Bullet	79
Tequador	79
Tequila Driver	79
Tequila Maria	79
Tequila Mockingbird	80
Tequila Rose	80
Tequila Quencher	80
Tequila Slider	80
Tequila Sunrise	80
Tequila Sunset	80
Test-Tube Baby	80
Tiajuana Bulldog	80
Tiajuana Screw	80
Tiajuana Split	80
Tiajuana Sunrise	81
T. K. O.	81
Tool	82
Toreador	82
Tuaca Margarita	52
White Bull	85
Wiki Waki Woo	86
TIA MARIA	
Alice in Wonderland	4
A.M.F.	5
Bam Be	7
Bikini Line	9
Black Jamaican	9
Blast from the Past	10
Blow Job (2)	11
Brahma Bull	13
Café Amore	16
Café Gates	16
Café Kingston	16
Café Reggae	17
Calypso Coffee	17
Cappa 21	18
Cappo de Tutti Cappi	18
Caribe Sunset	19
Cartel Buster	19
Chambord Repose	19
Deep Throat	24

Dirty Harry	25
Dry Arroyo	26
French Dream	30
Hunter's Coffee	36
Irish Maria	39
Jamaica Me Crazy (1)	40
Jamaican Coffee	40
Jamaican Dust	40
Jamaican Holiday	40
Jamaican Shake	41
Louvre Me Alone	46
Midway Rat	56
Mocha Jamocha	56
Montego Bay (1)	57
Mount Gay Café	58
Multiple Orgasm	58
Peter Prescription	62
Premium White Russian	65
Rasta Man	66
Reggae Walker	67
Russian' About	70
Sex on the Beach (1)	73
Sovereignty	76
Tender Mercies	79
Tour de Panama	82
Trophy Room	82
Voodoo Shooter	87
TUACA	
Black Ruby	9
Chicago Times	20
Forever Amber	29
Lemon Frappé	29
Hot Apple Pie	36
Nina's Coffee	59
Tender Mercies	79
Thumper	80
Tuaca Gimlet	32
Tuaca Margarita	52
Tuaca Pousse Café	65
VERMOUTH, DRY	
Affinity Cocktail	3
Boston Martini	52
Brainstorm Cocktail	14
Brazil	14
Bronx	14
Brooklyn	14
Buckeye Martini	52
Byrrh Cocktail	15
Cajun King Martini	52
Cajun Martini	52
Coronation	23
Diablo	25
Dry Brandy Manhattan	48
Dry Gibson	31
Dry Manhattan	48
Dry Martini	52
Dry Rob Roy	68
Dry Vodka Martini	52
Dutch Martini	52
Extra Dry Gibson	31
Extra Dry Martini	52
Extra Dry Vodka Martini	53
French Martini	53
Gibson	31
Gloomraiser	32
Half & Half	34
Hasta La Vista, Baby	35
Hot Martini	53
Ideal Cocktail	38
Klondike	44
Knockout	44